THE WAY
OF TANKA

THE WAY OF TANKA

Naomi Beth Wakan

Shanti Arts Publishing
Brunswick, Maine

THE WAY OF TANKA

Published by Shanti Arts Publishing

Cover and interior design by Shanti Arts Designs

Shanti Arts LLC
Brunswick, Maine
www.shantiarts.com

*Please note: "Haiku" and "tanka" are used for both singular and
plural forms. All poems are printed with permission of the authors;
in the event of an oversight, please contact the author or publisher
and proper acknowledgment will be made in forthcoming
editions. Poems not attributed are by Naomi Beth Wakan.*

Cover image by Christine Brooks Cote

Printed in the United States of America

First Edition

ISBN: 978-1-941830-60-4 (softcover)

ISBN: 978-1-941830-61-1 (digital)

LCCN: 2017933986

To Eli, tanka are the poems of love and nostalgia, and in them I can speak of my love for you and my appreciation of our many years together.

My thanks to my teacher, Sonja Arntzen, for helping me grow in tanka and allowing me to reprint here her very useful and lengthy introduction to the book we wrote together, *Double Take*.

CONTENTS

Tanka of exile

in exile
we make myths
of our homeland
poised uncertain between
assimilation and return

searching for a home
other than in our own heart
is perilous
must we always keep
our suitcase packed?

our past
is layered thickly
with people and places . . .
only looking back can
we see patterns in the journey

we move
from one age
to another
our life from birth to death
a continual diaspora

the rich textures
of our lives entrap us
into believing
we are solid, when we are
just stitched lightly together

INTRODUCTION

AFTER MANY YEARS OF IMMERSION IN THE HAIKU WORLD, opening to tanka writing has been a revelation for me. The pure sense images that I used in so disciplined a way in my haiku writing now were broken open to allow me to make use of metaphor, simile, allusion to the past, musings on the future, and all kinds of philosophical statements. Matters that could only be heard in the overtones and resonances of the haiku could now go directly on the page. This transformation has been guided by the eminent scholar of Japanese classical literature Sonja Arntzen, who encouraged my first attempts at tanka writing by example and support.

My interpretations and opinions expressed in *The Way of Tanka* may be considered entirely wrong by more learned experts, yet they may also be a fresh way of looking at tanka by an outsider venturing in. When it comes to the writing of tanka in English, just as the Japanese in the past have seized and adapted non-Japanese ideas in so many brilliant ways, perhaps it is possible for non-Japanese poets to seize and run with tanka in new directions. I sincerely hope this is so. Tanka is, after all, still defining itself. Denis M. Garrison expressed so well the general rules for writing any kind of poetry, though having tanka firmly in mind, when he wrote, "It is a delicate balance that one must strike. One must not discard the past in ignorance, but one also must not be constrained by the past. One must assiduously study the rules of poetics and then ignore them. The rules of poetics are not for writing the poem; the rules are for forming the craft of the poet. Every time a poet puts pen to paper, poetry is reinvented — or should be." In light of this quote, let's see what rules we should obey and then forget when it comes to the art of writing tanka.

when reading
a book of tanka
I'm surprised
at how many ways there are
to say "I'm lonely"

TAKE A LOOK

APART FROM PARENTS, THE MOST IMPORTANT PERSON IN the education of a child is the kindergarten teacher. It is this teacher who introduces the child to ways of learning. When a child is asked to take a picture of a house and color it within the lines, or is asked to draw a picture of a house with no guidance, or is asked to draw anything that interests them, the child is introduced to an experience that will impact the way he or she will learn in the future. The kindergarten teacher can show a child the exact route to take or can open a child to the necessity of questioning and the excitement of exploration. Children can be given set rules and nothing more, but the result may simply be obedience, or worse, inhibitions and boredom.

All this is to say that I am the kind of writing teacher who lets her students plunge in unknowingly and allows them the freedom of an untutored initial exploration of the matter in hand. Therefore, as this book is an introduction to tanka, I am not going to tell you, at this point, what is and is not a tanka; rather, I will offer you fifty examples of tanka that I love. These I hope you will read carefully and then try to sort out for yourself the kinds of ideas and feelings these five-liners are expressing, and how the brilliant tanka writers I have chosen have managed to pull this off so well in such a limited space.

remember when
we picked green plums
young and impatient
we never waited
for the ripening

    – Carole MacRury

spring yard work —
together we turn the earth
turn the worms . . .
the roots of our marriage
both forgiving and deep

    – Carole MacRury

spring magnolia
so short this time of deep
pink blooming . . .
yet we pick to own
what we'll soon discard

    – Carole MacRury

"mum, don't you
recognise my voice
any more" —
I blame the connection
but the truth is worst

    – Amelia Fielden

seniors' outing —
becoming aware that
I've entered
the time zone where death parts
more often than divorce

    − Amelia Fielden

how is it that ducks
are able to stay afloat
out on the water,
while I feel myself sinking
even here on land?

    − Fujiwara no Shunzei, translated by Steven D. Carter

our life in this world
is like the image one sees
inside a mirror —
something that's not really there,
but then not really not there.

    − Minamoto no Sanetomo, translated by Steven D. Carter

how I wish
my tanka of passion
did not erupt
solely from old memories —
last night's storm is over

    − Amelia Fielden

even in fog
the wild geese know
the way south —
for that kind of certainty
I would risk a short life

   — Jeanne Emrich

grinding
a handful of coffee beans
I enjoy
this time of not chasing
this time of not being chased

   — Reiko Hakozaki, translated by Kozue Uzawa and Amelia Fielden

the young brother
and sister on the see-saw
shrieking with joy
are alternately
summoned into the sky

   — Kiyomi Sato, translated by Kozue Uzawa and Amelia Fielden

"my mini garden
of crocuses and snowdrops
tiny though lovely"
first haiku I ever wrote
now tanka of nostalgia

   — Stephanie Bolster

the years pass
yearning to fly free
love holds me still —
yachts moored near the pier
move just a little

– Amelia Fielden

what shall we grow
this Year of the Ox
I want to seed
the entire valley
in meadowlarks

– Michael McClintock

if only the world would
always remain this way
some fishermen
drawing a little boat
up the river bank

– Minamoto no Sanetomo, translated by Sam Hamill

family album
decades of smiling faces
chart generations —
not one of us brave enough
to photograph the tears

– Beverley George

wanting my old life
when I wanted
my present life
stirring the soup she made
as a cold rain falls outside

  — Tom Clausen

one at a time
I step on stones
and cross the stream —
when I'm across, the stones
go back to what they were doing

  — Michael McClintock

expectations
strange to still have some
I search
garage sales for wedding rings
you might have given me

  — Kathy Kituai

if I squeezed
into a little box . . .
would you faint
when the postman
brought me to your door?

  — Kirsty Karkow

curtains move
shadows across the sill —
I look up
as though you were there
hoping I'd be here

   – Kathy Kituai

"too young
to really be in love"
now too old
to stay awake all night —
where did the between go?

   – Amelia Fielden

the two mating flies
on the deck feet up
I, the ruthless
slayer of generations
sip green tea

   – George Swede

might the sea clams
live dreaming in their shells?
like us in ours
might they also dream large?
I wonder, placing one in a pail

   – Michael McClintock

hilly paths
I walk where
once I ran —
sometimes the past
must be enough

  – Amelia Fielden

shimmering
on the desert track
a mirage
her smile radiant
for the man behind me

  – Rodney Williams

how utterly vain!
the great old men of China
arguing reason
before they can articulate
the origin of things

  – Motōri Norinaga, translated by Sam Hamill

once only
my heart whispered
this is love . . .
the astonishing simplicity
in just being together

  – Melissa Dixon

with the promotion
a corner office—
two window reflections
now vie for
my attention

   – George Swede

I dance by myself
to an old favorite
on the radio —
my shadow seems
older than I

   – George Swede

entering old age
I look less for truth
but find it more —
a mid-winter thaw reveals
pieces of sky

   – George Swede

wondering for years
what would be
my life's defining moment
      an egret staring at me
      me staring back

   – Jeanne Emrich

her plane disappears
into starlight . . .
and somewhere
in her luggage
my love poem

  – Michael Dylan Welch

writing a poem
of longing for her
I'm irritated
by the interruption
of her phone call

  – George Swede

in morning fog
we ship the oars and drift
between loon calls
all that's left of this world
the warmth of our bodies

  – Christopher Herold

as if she feels
how much I am missing you
already
a girl near me on the plane
begins to weep

  – Laura Maffei

barefoot
on warm sand
my toes
inches from the whole
Atlantic Ocean

    – Art Stein

thinking about it,
what else is there but this —
birth, death
and something in between
of uncertain duration?

    – Karma Tenzing Wangchuk

department meeting:
while the mouths utter business
the eyes ripple with
someone sailing, someone fishing,
someone drowning

    – George Swede

a sudden loud noise
all the pigeons of Venice
at once fill the sky
that is how it felt when your hand
accidentally touched mine

    – Ruby Spriggs

in love
you die of love
have talent
you die of talent
name it, you die

– Takuboku Ishikawa, translated by Carl Sesar

walking at night
along the sea
I feel like a coconut
washed up
from nowhere

– Takuboku Ishikawa, translated by Carl Sesar

never even noticed
the misspellings
then —
an old
love letter

– Takuboku Ishikawa, translated by Carl Sesar

wrote GREAT
in the sand
a hundred times
forgot about dying
and went on home

– Takuboku Ishikawa, translated by Carl Sesar

another day
of waking to the scent
of sea wrack . . .
ready to face the ebbs,
slacks and tidal surges

    – Carole MacRury

during the night
winds and a high tide
take the bottom step
what else might be lost
when my eyes are closed

    – Susan Constable

a toothpick
stuck into the cake
comes out clean . . .
wishing it were as easy
to know when I've said enough

    – Susan Constable

Christmas carols
on the radio —
my aunt Ida Rose
sings along
in Yiddish

    – Audrey Olberg

a shy child
my son would not walk too far
without permission
today he married a girl
I met at the wedding

— Joyce S. Greene

when you opened
my letter
were you surprised
my heart
flew out?

— Michael McClintock

Writing a tanka

Writing a tanka
is like feeling
the breeze coming up
from the shore
on the first day of Autumn.
It tells you that
the full blooming of summer
is over —
the seeds sown in Spring
are now to be harvested,
and entropy moves center stage
as leaves fall and
stalks rot in the ground.
Yes, writing tanka
is like that.
Like a record of a full life
and the bitter-sweetness
of knowing that
it must come to an end.

SO WHAT DO WE HAVE HERE?

I wonder what struck you when you read those
fifty tanka? Of course, you would have immediately seen
that they are all five lines long and the lengths of the lines
follow a pattern: *short, long, short, long, long*. Tanka,
when written in Japanese, have a structure of 5, 7, 5, 7, 7,
which we think of as the number of syllables per line, but
these are actually the number of *on*, or sound units. The
Japanese language structure is not at all similar to English,
so this count has no bearing for poets writing tanka in
English. If one doesn't keep somewhat to the *short, long,
short, long, long* length of lines, however, the tanka
becomes little distinguishable from short free verse. The
last tanka, by Michael McClintock [page 25], is an example
of an extremely brief tanka, often called minimalist tanka. A
few tanka writers in English stay with the Japanese count of
thirty-one syllables, probably for the discipline. Some prefer
minimalist style — around nineteen. But most tanka writers
choose to stay somewhere in between. However, a good
reminder comes from Michael Dylan Welch, who said, "It's
the poetry that counts," rather than the syllables.

You may have noticed that over half of these tanka have
strong sense images. Jane Reichhold calls this "giving the
mind a picture." Sight is in fact the most frequently used
sense, and tanka poets use strong metaphors to express
what they notice, as in the following tanka by Susan
Constable. As a poet of the domestic scene, I find her choice
of metaphor quite interesting:

a toothpick
stuck into the cake
comes out clean . . .
wishing it were as easy
to know when I've said enough

Other strong visual images are given by Beverley George:

family album
decades of smiling faces
chart generations —
not one of us brave enough
to photograph the tears

and Rodney A. Williams:

shimmering
on the desert track
a mirage
her smile radiant
for the man behind me

As for the sense of hearing, I am so amused by Aunt Ida Rose. Note that, although five lines, this is an irregular tanka to the usual form:

Christmas carols
on the radio—
my aunt Ida Rose
sings along
in Yiddish

    – Audrey Olberg

For the sense of smell, we have this by Carole MacRury:

another day
of waking to the scent
of sea wrack . . .
ready to face the ebbs,
slacks and tidal surges

And for touch, here is a much reproduced tanka by a fine poet, Ruby Spriggs, alas, now dead:

a sudden loud noise
all the pigeons of Venice
at once fill the sky
that is how it felt when your hand
accidentally touched mine

For taste, we have a witty tanka by the green-tea-drinking poet George Swede:

the two mating flies
on the deck feet up
I, the ruthless
slayer of generations
sip green tea

In the Heian period (794 – 1185), a prosperous time in Japanese history for poetry and literature, tanka were used for communication, especially between lovers. You may have noticed the many beautiful love tanka included in the selection of fifty tanka, for example, this by Michael Dylan Welch:

her plane disappears
into starlight . . .
and somewhere
in her luggage
my love poem

and Carole MacRury's tanka on mature love:

spring yard work —
together we turn the earth
turn the worms . . .
the roots of our marriage
both forgiving and deep

The theme of love is often present, whether it be joyous remarks about new love or nostalgia for past love, as in this tanka by Amelia Fielden:

how I wish
my tanka of passion
did not erupt
solely from old memories —
last night's storm is over

Of course, philosophical musings are frequent in tanka:

in love
you die of love
have talent
you die of talent
name it, you die

— Takuboku Ishikawa, translated by Carl Sesar

thinking about it
what else is there but this —
birth, death
and something in between
of uncertain duration?

— Karma Tenzing Wangchuk

Many tanka have two parts: the first is often the setting of the scene, and the last part, generally the last two lines, is a comment that expands the personal to the universal, or vice versa. If the reflection is deep enough, what applies to one person's moment can become a truth for all of us, as in this tanka by Christopher Herold:

> in morning fog
> we ship the oars and drift
> between loon calls
> all that's left of this world
> the warmth of our bodies

The occasional tanka is merely one long flow:

> how utterly vain!
> the great old men of China
> arguing reason
> before they can articulate
> the origin of things
>
> — Motōri Norinaga, translated by Sam Hamill

Tanka can overflow with metaphor and simile. Takuboku Ishikawa was a highly original Japanese tanka poet who totally refreshed the tanka scene with his startling images and ideas:

walking at night
along the sea
I feel like a coconut
washed up
from nowhere

    – Takuboku Ishikawa, translated by Carl Sesar

Another example of metaphor, by George Swede, parallels truths appearing from nowhere with the clear sky that breaks through the grey of winter:

entering old age
I look less for truth
but find it more —
a mid-winter thaw reveals
pieces of sky

There is also this wonderful tanka by Amelia Fielden, in which her attempts to "fly free" are compared to the shifting of an anchored boat:

the years pass
yearning to fly free
love holds me still —
yachts moored near the pier
move just a little

Sometimes the whole tanka is just a thoughtful question, as in this witty piece by Kirsty Karkow:

if I squeezed
into a little box . . .
would you faint
when the postman
brought me to your door?

You will surely have noticed that there are no titles, no capitalization (except where proper names are used), and little punctuation. Tanka aren't usually thought of as complete sentences, and leaving the beginning word without a capital letter — indicating a continuation of where they've come from — and the end word without a following period — indicating where things are going — allows the reader to enter into the open tanka with their imagination on the ready. I like Denis M. Garrison's description of tanka as just "the middle of the story."

PIVOT LINES AND LAST LINES

DURING MY YEARS AS A THERAPIST, I BECAME PAINFULLY aware of the gap between what people wanted to express and what they were able to express: the chasm between inner and outer lives. Later in life, when I gave a series of writing workshops, I came across that same division again, almost a barrier between what budding writers wanted to tell the world and the words they actually put down on paper. These folks, even though committed to expressing their ideas, had trouble linking their inner and outer selves.

These periods in my life came yet once more into my consciousness as I started to consider the function of the pivot line in tanka. The pivot line is usually the third of the five lines, and its function is to link the outer image, whatever has alerted the tanka poet, to his or her inner thoughts and emotions that have arisen from the image. In other words, the pivot is between the emotion and what caused the emotion:

> *December sunrise*
> *even the usual crows*
> *absolutely still*
> *this brief moment between*
> *the in-breath and the out-breath*
>
> — Kirsty Karkow

Just as the therapist can help the client bridge the gap between inner turmoil and outer behavior, and as the writing coach can encourage the would-be writer to leap the barrier inhibiting their words spilling out on paper, so tanka poets are able to bridge the outer image they have sensed with the feelings and thoughts that have arisen from that sensing. For the tanka poet, the tool is the pivot line, which takes one from observation to introspection, links Heaven and Earth, as it were. When inside blends with outside in this way, I call it integrity.

This link, this pivot, as I said earlier, is often the third line of the tanka. In a way, it is hanging in the air so the poet can use it to swing from objective to subjective mood, or vice versa. To fulfill its function, therefore, the pivot line must make sense when read with the first two lines as well as when read as a precursor to the last two lines. In other words, the pivot line means one thing as a finish to the first couple of lines and something else as a herald to the last two lines. By this linking, both the initial image and the reaction to it are not just joined, but are taken to deeper depths, and the full five lines resonate more fully with unexpected harmonies. The pivot line adds a richness to each section as well as revealing their connection.

The pivot line, therefore, acts rather as the volta line in sonnets. The sonnet's ninth line, linking the octet to the last five lines, joins the situation presented at the beginning with a kind of resolution at the end. The volta, as the pivot line, allows for a change of mood, a change of position, even a change of topic at the end of the sonnet.

To illustrate the pivot line, let's consider this tanka by
Francine Porad:

> a woman
> holds a waving child high
> as the train passes
> where . . . when . . .
> did summer disappear

The woman and child in this tanka do not have an
obvious connection with summer until the line describing
something passing speedily, "the train," is introduced. It
links the two topics perfectly as the train passing speedily
past the mother and child is compared with summer
passing speedily in the consciousness of the writer, and
may also be subtly suggesting that childhood moves to
adulthood too fast.

Here is another tanka with a pivot line worth some attention.
The night airplane links the ear and the stars, which feel,
paradoxically, closer than the plane.

> just out of earshot
> the periodic blinking
> of a night airplane,
> not quite far enough away
> to be as close as the stars
>
> — Gerald St. Maur

Sometimes there are two pivot moments, as in my tanka:

> wind from the beach
> what does it foretell?
> colors of autumn
> the falling away of desires
> as the winged-seeds fall.

The question in the second line is answered in the fourth line, but "colors of autumn" also swivels the tanka from "wind from the beach" to "winged seeds falling." So long as the five lines are all connected in some way, the pivot line can vary in position.

In the writing of tanka in Japanese, because there are so many homonyms in that language, the pivot line is often a pun. Even in tanka written in English, a pun can offer the needed twist:

> our cottage
> far from its neighbors
> lost in the pines . . .
> how I long for those days
> when my life was in order

The word "pine" offers the two meanings, "tree" and "longing for," that provide the necessary link. Oddly enough, the word for pine in Japanese, *matsu*, also means "longing for," and is often used in this way.

Even if the pivot line doesn't offer a pun, it should present something that twists the first image around or extends it in some way. Direct puns rarely occur in tanka written in English. Linkages, however, can occur by using carefully chosen words, as in this case where the operative word appears in the first line:

> jingle of the dog's collar
> out in the hall —
> we pause
> in our lovemaking,
> Christmas Eve
>
> — Michael Dylan Welch

Michael Dylan Welch explains his use of the word "jingle": "It's not quite the same as a pun, but here I want 'jingle' to have a double meaning — the literal meaning of the noise the dog's collar makes, and once we learn it's Christmas Eve, the suggested meaning of bells on Santa's suit. Hence the pause."

I'll finish with a few tanka that have clear, strong pivot lines that I think work well. In the first tanka below, the words "tangled in vines" link the image of Snow White with the tanka writer, who feels, for a brief moment, like Snow White, seemingly dead while being alive within the entanglement of her bedroom ivy, although this is entirely conjecture on my part.

Snow White
in her glass coffin
tangled in vines —
the bedroom ivy
nearly to my pillow

– Angela Leuck

In the next tanka, the word "empty" links the literal
emptiness of a cupboard when a person's clothes have
gone, indicating that the person also has gone, with a more
positive view of the word "empty" as a void full of potential.

your side
of the wardrobe
empty
I wait to be filled
with possibility

– David Terelinck

In this tanka by Tom Clausen, "between us" makes sense of
the first two lines and adds poignancy to the last two:

the cold walk
silence
between us
the creek running
under ice

In the following tanka, which appeared in the first chapter, "a mirage" completes what is shimmering on the desert track and also introduces the mistaken idea of Williams thinking her smile was for him.

> shimmering
> on the desert track
> a mirage
> her smile radiant
> for the man behind me
>
>   — Rodney A. Williams

The words "a staggering blow" is a perfect pivot line, linking the striking of the oak and the striking effect of the diagnosis.

> the brief cloud of snow
> as an axe strikes this oak
> a staggering blow
> after his diagnosis
> I can't hear the doctor's voice
>
>   — Denis M. Garrison

The next tanka, which also appeared in the first chapter, intrigues us as we ponder what Emrich has been wondering for years, which turns out to be the third line, "Life's defining moment." This latches on to the next two lines by explaining what the image of the egret was. This is a fine

example of a tanka with an interesting pivot line and a
surprise last line. Everything I could ask for.

> wondering for years
> what would be
> my life's defining moment
>   an egret staring at me
>   me staring back
>
> – Jeanne Emrich

Tanka do not need a pivot line, and it is often missing
in tanka in English. However, I feel the pivot line, by its
clever linking and its ability to segue, emphasizes the gaps
we have in so many parts of our lives and so deepens the
poignancy of our divisions.

Now to the last lines of tanka. I wonder whether it is only
me who demands a strong last line in a tanka. After all, a
tanka is a summing up of the universe — no matter how
mundane the subject — and it needs a punch to round
it off. I call it the rabbit's kick. A very well-known poet,
commenting on my poetry, once said it is really prose until
you come to the last line. Yes, somehow my last lines often
work to shift all the words before to give them a greater
impact and, indeed, to make the many lines before seem
a relevant part of a "real" poem. So it is with a tanka. As a
reader coming to the end of a tanka, I ask to be surprised,
shifted, or at least captured with some moment of interest or

some moment of questioning. I don't want my response to be: "So what?" A strong last line can help achieve what I am looking for.

In Japanese textiles, it has been noted that the design and the ground are carefully worked together. If the design is too faint, the ground will dominate. If, on the other hand, the design is too cluttered and complex, the ground will seem unessential. If the ground weaving is too strong a color or too marked a texture, the design will suffer. This is also the case when it comes to Japanese tanka collections. The Japanese feel that if the poems are all consistently good, none will stand out. By having the occasional brilliant poem against a background of reasonably good ones, it will seem even more startling, I suppose.

This idea is completely alien to Western poets who require that each poem in a collection have distinction. I, myself, can't see why I would have a collection where only some poems hit their target and the others wavered. I want an anthology to be the best it can be, and usually, in Western collections, that is, in fact, what they are called: *The Best of . . .*

Perhaps the Japanese are more aware of the need for contrast; after all, life is both laughter and tears. In haiku, the two images juxtaposed are often of something far away and something nearby, something large and something small. This pulling of the universal down into the everyday is a characteristic of Japanese tanka and haiku. In the West, we want to dwell on heavenly clouds all the while. We want all our apples to look perfect, all our children to turn out well, and all the tanka in our collections to be top-notch. Japanese, on the other hand find reading endless "perfect" tanka boring; twenty percent excellent would be plenty for most Japanese readers.

I don't favor the peaks and valleys Japanese prefer in tanka collections. Just as I espouse the idea that "either it is a haiku, or it isn't," so I tend to feel that way about tanka too. I want each tanka to send me spinning. I realize a mundane recording of everyday life is capable of revealing a universal truth, but it will more likely, I think, read like a diary entry. These days, as tanka is becoming increasingly popular, I seem to read whole books and magazines of them without giving that sigh, or that "Aha!" that I continually want. Recently, I read a copy of a magazine that contained two hundred and seventy tanka. I marked ten that really caught my attention. That seems way too few, even for a peaks-and-valleys theory. I recognize that no one's life is a perpetual high, so why should a book of tanka be? Yet, I still ask for that. Perhaps, at my age, I need quick fixes of insight, but it seems that far too many tanka books and magazines read like dull diaries when it seems they ought to be filled with things that poets urgently need to say.

To be fair, however, I like to look at the opposite side's case in such situations, so maybe if I tried to look deeper into each tanka instead of skimming through them for winners, as is my usual wont when I am reading, I might find what I am looking for. Sanford Goldstein, who writes at least ten tanka every day, speaks of those everyday tanka as "spilling" out of him. So perhaps everyday tanka do serve a purpose.

Here are a few tanka with strong last lines that delighted and surprised me and left me totally satisfied. In the first one, the last line links the baby to Batman's need to save mankind and reminds us of the enormity of such a task.

Halloween —
infant Batman
in my arms
barely aware of this world
that needs saving

    — Laura Maffei

novice gardener
religiously I water
my little patch
and lo! on the evening
of the third day . . . radishes

    — Linda Papanicolaou

Here is a tanka by Michael McClintock with a nice little ending that starts by echoing one of Robert Frost's famous poems. I was expecting some kind of profound decision but got a basic need instead:

> two roads diverged
> off the Golden State
> . . . I chose
> the one that goes
> by Taco Bell

I'd like to finish this chapter by returning to the pivot line and quoting a much reproduced piece by Gerald St. Maur on the shifts that occur in tanka, often guided by that line: "In going beyond the experience of the moment, the tanka takes us from delight to fulfillment, from insight to comprehension, and from psycho-orgasm to love, in general from the spontaneous to the measured. To achieve this requires a fundamental shift in emphasis: from glimpse to gaze, from first sight to exploration, and from juxtaposition to interplay; in short, from awareness to perspective."

Tanka on diagnosis

in the clinic waiting-room
we catch up on gossip
laughing in companionship
forgetting for a moment
a possible feared diagnosis

on diagnosis
time changed for her
each moment
became the only one and
each space stretched to the horizon

as pain
invaded her life
and only then
she realized a certain meaning
that gave sense to nonsense

plans and goals
disappeared with fatigue
all that was left . . .
a vague sense of self and
of the seasons passing

all she knew
was one anxiety
the anxiety
that maybe she had never been true
true to herself that is

TANKA REVIEW

As we begin to get a feel for tanka, let's pause and review a few of the things we have already noticed. For me, tanka written in English must still reflect something of what characterizes a tanka in Japanese. For this reason, I would define a tanka as a five-line poem of various line lengths, but preferably of the *short, long, short, long, long* form, resembling somewhat the form of *waka*, the original name for tanka. The contents may be of any topic, but the most common is that of a sensual image, often taken from nature, and some comment on it that reflects human nature or the state of the universe.

But a tanka isn't just a five-line poem of roughly nineteen to thirty-one syllables. Unfortunately, as I try to explain what makes a tanka a tanka, I find it almost undefinable, for tanka seem to me to be the poetry of ephemeralness, of dissatisfaction, of longings never fulfilled. Tanka have a certain tone — always a hard thing to pin down. But to me, the most important feature of a tanka is the rabbit's foot kick that often occurs in the last line because it defines, basically summarizes, all that has gone before, and gives the reader the jolt in perspective that opens their lives to other possibilities.

Remember this tanka?

> *what shall we grow*
> *this Year of the Ox?*
> *I want to seed*
> *the entire valley*
> *in meadowlarks*
>
> — Michael McClintock

We are expecting crops, but we get a surprise: meadowlarks.

Some tanka, as we have seen, seem to be one or a series of images cascading down from line to line, but others seem to consist clearly of two parts linked with a pivot line.

Remember, within a mere five lines, tanka can almost catch and almost define the universe, and if we poets can do that, it is too good a chance to miss. Did I mention that tanka is one of the world's oldest continually written poetry forms? Just think what a lineage you will be carrying on when you start to write your own tanka.

Four tanka on "haiku"

I have stood
in Bashō's birthplace
in Iga Ueno
longing for some inspiration
to rise from the dirt floor

I have just read
of Bashō's wife
(albeit common-law)
why in his thousands of haiku
did he not once tell of his love?

Shiki
a breath of fresh air
for haiku
a breath of fresh air
for Shiki

being
one himself
how could Issa
not be one with all underdogs . . .
the authenticity of his words

TANKA COMPARED WITH HAIKU

Tanka is not a stretched haiku! —Michael Dylan Welch

AS MANY POETS COME TO TANKA VIA THE WRITING OF haiku, I think it is opportune here to compare haiku and tanka and see what we are dealing with when we decide to express ourselves in five lines rather than three.

It might be best to start this chapter with definitions of both haiku and tanka to see what we are exploring; and believe me, there are almost as many definitions of the two as there are writers. Here are my rough definitions, and please be aware that I am discussing present day, written-in-English haiku and tanka.

Haiku are brief poems consisting of two or more everyday sense images juxtaposed in a way that not only define the moment, but define it so penetratingly that each image is augmented by the other. To add to the definition of tanka covered in the previous chapter, here are useful words from Denis M. Garrison: "tanka are untitled, unrhymed quintain." Certainly we can agree on that, but please allow me a second shot at my previous definition to say that tanka are five-line poems that move from image to image, idea to idea, feeling to feeling, yet the whole five lines flow together seamlessly to present a strong statement of humanity's place in the universe, even though the poem may be intensely personal.

Many descriptions of tanka could easily be applied to haiku, and yet, haiku and tanka are very different forms of poetry. Haiku is immediate, and tanka is nostalgic and reflective. This difference, I believe, is because of their original sources. Haiku derived from the first three lines of *renga*, a poetry game that has been around for some five hundred years. For renga, a group of poets sit around creating spontaneously linked lines of poetry. The first poet offers three lines, the next poet gives two lines, and the third three lines. The three-and-two-line alternation continues around the group of gathered poets until the end of the renga is reached. While this could be after hundreds of sections, most renga finish after thirty-six, a *kasen*.

Of course there are rules to the game. Certain sections must or must not address certain subjects, such as the seasons or other aspects of nature. Also, to start the poetry writing session, the first three lines are usually offered by the most distinguished poet present; poets would often prepare "spontaneous" lines ahead of time in hopes of being asked to begin the poem. Usually the first three lines would state when and where the meeting was taking place and also something that attracted the lead poet's attention at the moment of writing. As the focus was the immediate present, those first three lines were always written in the present tense. Eventually, the first three lines split off and became a poetry form in their own right, as haiku.

Haiku as a separate poetry form has been around for four hundred years. Tanka, on the other hand, is over thirteen hundred years old. Tanka were originally lyric poems with an oral history that reaches back to the eighth century C.E. These early musical chantings, derived from *uta* (songs), were known as *waka*. *Wa* is the oldest recorded name for Japan, and *waka* was the name given to poems in the Japanese style rather than the Chinese style, which had been dominant up to that time. One of the early collections, the *Man'yōshū*, contained four thousand waka. Some of these waka stood alone, and some of them acted as a coda to longer poems being written at this time, namely *choka*. These waka were actually a kind of summing up of what had gone before, a reflection, a gathering of thoughts on the subject covered. For this reason, tanka can be written in the past tense, the present tense, or even be a projection into the future; they can be philosophical, meditative, or critical; and they can involve all kinds of thoughts and emotions.

Haiku speak only of things sensed in the present, and they concern only sense objects: what is being seen, smelled, tasted, touched, and heard. Traditionally, these sense objects were confined to observations about nature: cherry blossoms, mist, mountains; more recently: the smell of cooking, the touch of a baby's skin. Haiku never directly state emotions or ideas. They never make moral judgments or philosophical comments. They just stay with what is being sensed at a moment in time. Haiku is the poetry of nouns — strong nouns, nouns that may suggest and imply ideas and feelings but never express them overtly. It is as though haiku expound William Carlos William's outlook: "No truth but in things."

Tanka, on the other hand, is more the poetry of verbs.

They cover any subject and are contemplative, offering ideas to be considered, such as the meaning of reality and comments on the human experience from birth to death. Feelings and ideas are spoken of directly in tanka, and if sense objects are dwelt on at all, the focus is on their significance in the ways of the world. The information provided by tanka is not only more than that offered by haiku, but of a different nature, and therein, I think, lies the essential difference between haiku and tanka. Tanka view a subject from many angles, whereas haiku are usually concerned with the essence of a sensation, the "isness" of it, the immediate connection, beyond words. Tanka lead to contemplation, whereas haiku offer the "Aha!" of intuitive understanding.

Haiku are concerned with sense objects and so speak of things as they are; they are objective. Tanka, on the other hand, are a consideration of things, and can speak of the beautiful, ugly, evil, and good. Tanka, being subjective, tend to be reflective, and the poet often makes judgmental statements. Tanka poets notice what they are going to write about and then, distancing themselves from it, are able to comment on their topic. Whereas, in haiku, it is as if the poet has blended with the subject, and only the subject remains. Although haiku depend on an intense personal sensing of the moment, the first person pronouns — "I" or "we" — rarely appear; whereas tanka, also personal statements in which one can hear the writer's voice in the lines, often use such pronouns.

Consider the haiku and tanka below, both set in cottage country:

> empty cabin
> the beached canoe
> fills with leaves
>
>   — Devar Dahl

> in the morning fog
> we slip our oars and drift
> between loon calls
> all that's left of this world
> the warmth of our bodies
>
>   — Christopher Herold

The haiku speaks only of images: an empty cabin, a canoe filled with leaves. Yet, on consideration, it is clear to us that this haiku clearly speaks of the impermanence of things, using just those images with no overt indication of this inner idea. The tanka also has strong sense images: the drifting boat, the loon's call, but it allows itself a comment that directs our thoughts to the high value of human contact in a cold world.

Tanka, as I have mentioned, became the poetry of the Heian Court. Tanka (then called waka) was the poetry between lovers having secret assignations; it was the poetry of patron and patronized; the poetry of elegance. Haiku, on the other hand, was neither the poetry of the court nor of the warrior. Haiku was the poetry of the common man; the poetry of the everyday; of simplicity; of pumping water and chopping wood. Haiku, when liberated from renga, tended to be adopted by merchants and lower classes as their chosen form of poetry writing.

If one subject predominates in tanka, it is human love, mostly unrequited. Haiku, on the other hand, uses nature as a hidden metaphor for the ways of mankind. Tanka tells of human beings and their goings-on directly. Of course haiku can occasionally be about humans and tanka occasionally about nature, but the basic distinction, at least in traditional-style writing, is that haiku is concerned with the natural world, and tanka dwells on the human condition. Here, just to show it can be done, is a haiku concerned with the human condition and a tanka based on nature:

removal van
pulls away already cold
fills the room

    – Jeffry Harpeng

slanted sun
of late autumn
paints
the dry grass
burnished gold

    – Mary Mageau

Regarding images, a haiku usually has two that are juxtaposed to imply a contrast, a similarity, or an association that allows the reader to extrapolate the feelings and thoughts that resonate from the given objects. Tanka can have as many as five images, one per line, or it can be one long image flowing through the five lines.

In traditional haiku-writing, and also in those written in English, the most ordinary, everyday simple words are used to describe what is being sensed. Traditional Japanese tanka use more symbolically-powered words that, because of Japan's homogeneous society, would immediately be understood by the cultured reader. Even when written in English, tanka tend to have a more complex vocabulary than do haiku.

Haiku, when attached as the first lines of renga, had to be immediate, for in renga-writing, poets were waiting to pick up the lines created and add their own. There was no time for simile or metaphor. One couldn't pause to consider how this is like that; the idea was to tell how this is like this. Tanka could be produced more slowly because there was a lot to be considered: how to word a love letter to entrance the recipient, how to write to a famous monk to proclaim respect for him, how to record your own insights. So, tanka have room for metaphor, simile . . . in fact, the whole kitchen sink.

One can use one's imagination when writing tanka; one can let one's mind float to other times and places. Haiku have to stay with the immediate sense object/s. Haiku have to hit the target directly, whereas tanka have room to jump to the ends of the universe before coming to the point.

One should not think that haiku are without depth, however, for by concentrating on the here and now, the poet can actually reveal universal truths that will reverberate and resonate as the haiku is read. Tanka is concerned with human joys and woes, and often, at least in traditional tanka, speak explicitly of the four Noble Truths of Buddhism: all is suffering; one suffers because one is attached and has cravings; such cravings can be stilled; and one can accomplish this by following the path of right living, right speech, right occupation, etc. Tanka remind us constantly that all is ephemeral.

Below are a haiku and a tanka that both speak of the unsatisfactoriness of human relations, here defined by the family:

family visit
he tries to fix what's wrong
with the answering machine

    – Winona Baker

family album
decades of smiling faces
chart generations —
not one of us brave enough
to photograph the tears

    – Beverley George

Both poems are concerned with communication within families, but only the tanka has room to spell it out explicitly. Yet, both are equally strong in their power to convey the message.

A tanka is more than a haiku plus two lines, however. The authority on haiku and tanka, Michael Dylan Welch, was quoted at the beginning of this chapter: "Tanka are not just stretched haiku." When reciting haiku and tanka, it is not one breath versus two breaths that make the difference.

To accentuate what has already been said, in a satisfactory haiku, the subject and object are fused; the archer, arrow, and target become one, and the "I" disappears into the moment. In tanka, the writer is separated from the subject, pulled back from it, and so can discuss it in an objective manner, giving opinions, expressing feelings, making moral judgments, waxing philosophical. The tanka writer and the subject matter are two different entities. There is no room for such separation in haiku.

Tanka can recall the past, drum up the future, as well as deal with the present. It can be filled with simile and metaphor; in fact, some tanka are just one long metaphor. Tanka can call up imaginary scenes, use awkward and unusual words. Tanka can do anything so long as it is contained in five lines. Yet the lingering overtones, as I mentioned earlier, are the same in both tanka and haiku: the ephemeralness of life, the awesomeness of the universe, the smallness of man, the sense that life is too sweet to leave and yet too bitter to cling to.

The following two poems cover the same subject, but the haiku implies the degree of sadness with the words "autumn rain," whereas the tanka spells out that the writer fears that "the truth is worse."

it's happened
my mother doesn't know me
autumn rain

  — Winona Baker

"mum don't
you recognize my voice
any more?"
I blame the connection
but the truth is worse

  — Amelia Fielden

Consider these two as well:

bumper cars
all facing the same way
summer's end

  — Dan McCullough

end of summer
a bikini-top pinned
to the notice-board
all that's left of the hoards
filling the park a week ago

— Naomi Beth Wakan

Haiku reached our shores long before tanka, and this is explained by Michael Dylan Welch: "A hundred years ago haiku appealed to the Imagists, who found in haiku something that validated their focus on images. Tanka didn't do that nearly so well. Sixty years ago, the Beat poets found in haiku something that echoed with their fascination with Zen (and we're still having to live down the idea that haiku is somehow a Zen art — which is mostly a Western notion). I do think tanka is already more of a Western style of poetry in what it allows, so it didn't have the novelty of haiku, which was more restricted in its techniques. Westerners could already write poetry that was like tanka, but not like haiku, so haiku was a more attractive novelty." I'd add to these reasons for tanka's delayed entry into the Western world the fact that most short poetry magazines only accepted haiku, and there were few outlets for tanka poets to see their works in print, and indeed, few to champion it.

Although tanka is overtly richer with its strong images and powerful emotions, a good haiku with full resonances can be just as strong. As Michael McClintock points out, "a haiku isn't a failed tanka, nor a tanka a failed haiku." They are just different ways to tell of things.

USES OF TANKA

Tanka are the perfect vehicle for capturing the swift, direct pulse of emotion. —Carl Sesar

The Uses of Tanka

In Heian times,
tanka were sweet confirmations
between courtier lovers
of deeds done and to be done.
And also of court rapists,
for dark chambers and
many-layers of kimono
hid identities, so seducers
were never quite sure that
they had entered the right woman.
Even in such cases of mistake,
the next morning the maiden
would receive a token tanka
speaking of her long hair perhaps,
and other matters, and it would be
attached to the prescribed branch
from say a flowering cherry.
She, in return, whether mad with anger,
sulking, or perhaps with a small smile,
would be obliged to also write a tanka,
in response, commenting on the situation,
and send it along with maybe
a late blooming plum blossom.

A few years later both women,
whether seduced, or once loved,
might be found writing more acerbic tanka
complaining of neglect, or at least
that the dwelling he had provided
for them was not up to par.
Tanka-writing would also be called for
when noblemen, at time of banishment,
(maybe for a political misstep, or
for the seduction of the Emperor's favorite)
thought sadly of the Capitol
they would be leaving for say
the beaches of Suma (always a good place
for writing mournful tanka of exile).
These days, I write tanka
when my haiku get uppity
with the conceit that they have
nailed the moment to the page.
I slap them with two extra lines,
reminding them that all things pass,
particularly the "here and now"
and even if things don't pass
as quickly as we would like,
it's all illusory anyway.
Yes, tanka are useful for times
such as these.

Skylight tanka, *celebrating our new skylight, handily situated above the daybed.*

high winds —
at the blink of an eye-lid
a new set of clouds
move swiftly across the skylight
restless skyscape, restless me

the sun rises
high above the solitary pine . . .
I decide
to lie and watch it
labor across the sky

grey skylight
grey trees viewed
through it
grey me looking at
all this greyness

today the clouds
are many-layered . . .
as a child
I would lie and wonder
if God lived above the highest

the sun explodes
on the skylight . . .
I get distracted
by the smears my bad cleaning
have left across the glass

VARIETIES OF TANKA

While tanka were primarily used for
correspondence between courtiers, lovers, and friends,
tanka were also written on important occasions, say at the
death of a notable person. It was also traditional in Japan to
write a poem close to the time of one's own death, and while,
later on, often haiku was the chosen form, tanka were also
used for this purpose:

> I wish to die
> in spring, beneath
> the cherry blossoms,
> while the springtime moon
> is full.
>
> — Saigyo (1190), quoted by Joseph Kirby

Tanka would be written at times of celebration, say
following the birth of a baby or moving into a new house.
As tanka writing was considered a necessary skill for a
cultured person, tanka competitions, when teams of poets
competed against each other, were frequent.

Often, traditional tanka would have as their first line a
reference to another literary work, for knowledge of past
literary efforts was much esteemed. I tried this myself
with a set of poems based on the writings of Krishnamurti,
inserting a line borrowed from him as the last line in each
tanka:

10 tanka for Krishnamurti
(the bold italic line is borrowed from Krishnamurti)

children
building a rocket-ship
with cardboard boxes
angels may fear to tread, but ah
the confidence of innocence

holding
her grandchild's hand
outside the zoo
she suddenly feels happy . . .
and lingers in the moment

lifting the rock
children shriek with delight
as hidden crabs scatter
the ringing of bells and eating of wafer
has nothing to do with searching

he looks closely
at a small wasps' nest
built in a cavity . . .
without awareness of things
most people are as good as dead

knowing the planet
is round is helpful for
truth-seekers
beginning here will return you here
there is no end to the journey

no matter
how many words we say
to each other
the essence lies in the spaces between
the essence lies in the pauses

why search
for gurus in haystacks
cleaning out your ears
alert to what they are saying?
it is you who has to understand life

wanting this
or that to happen
is futile
everything is set in jelly
ambitions breed anxiety

going to
the ends of the earth
is a waste of energy
hang around the homestead for
truth may be under a dead leaf

they watch admiringly
as the father quail supervises
his noisy offspring
while mother pecks at the clover
is not life an extraordinary thing?

This brings me to tanka collage, tanka montage, tanka string, tanka sequence, and other kinds of tanka. As defined by Michael McClintock, tanka collage is "an assemblage of tanka with other short forms . . . intended as an aesthetic whole," and tanka montage is "two or more tanka composed or arranged as a set, intended as an aesthetic whole." It was Sanford Goldstein who drew a distinction between tanka string and tanka sequence. He defines tanka string as "poems tied to a single subject. Ideally, all poems in a tanka string are connected at every point in the same way a string is connected infinitely by minuscule atoms." A tanka sequence, on the other hand, orders the stanzas in a chronological dramatic order. It is much more organized than a tanka string, having a beginning, a middle, and an end, and it often has a strong conclusion reflecting the state of the world. Each tanka is linked in some way to the tanka before it.

What follows is a tanka string with a common theme:

On Waking Tanka

on waking
in a shower of rain
my limbs
sink into the mattress
as if half-immersed in clay

on waking
on a sunny morning
my body
light as a rolling tumbleweed
springs eagerly towards the day

on waking
on a frosty morning
my mind
a stretched piece of glass through which
all can be seen clearly

on waking
in a snowfall
the whiteness
brings a new light into the bedroom
radiant, yet silent

on waking
in a dense fog
I lie suspended . . .
in the distance a ship's horn
sounds out a warning

Tanka can also be added to a brief prose paragraph, just as haiku are added to one to make *haibun*. The form is called tanka prose and predates haibun by many centuries. The tanka can come first and then the prose, or vice versa. It can even be a sandwich with a tanka in the middle of two pieces of prose, or prose between two tanka. Sanford Goldstein often uses this form. The prose can set the stage for the tanka, or the tanka can consolidate and enrich what is being said in the prose.

Here is an example of tanka prose by Patricia Prime that resonates with me because of my own wartime experiences in England:

The Cardboard Suitcase

Click of the Box Brownie. In the photo I clutch Mum with one hand; my other holds a toy dog on wheels.
As if it were yesterday, I see Dad in his khaki uniform, shouldering his kit bag as he waves and turns the corner. Mum, back in the kitchen, dissolves in tears when she discovers he's left his sugar ration lying on the table. She's waving goodbye to us a short time later. We're on the train with hundreds of other children for evacuation to the Midlands for the duration of the bombing. In my hands a cardboard suitcase and gas mask . . .

out of the dark
the mournful sound
of a train whistle —
the smell of black smoke
permeates the carriage

the suddenness
of being alone
and no one to care
a guard comforts me
with a sticky toffee

standing
over a puddle
rainbowed with oil
I make a wish
to see mum again

Many poets come to tanka via haiku, so there is a tendency to make the first three lines a haiku and then add two lines of comments. Michael McClintock used the label *taika* for this form of tanka and described it in this way: "[taika is] . . . a style of tanka construction that combines a three-line haiku in typical object language with two additional lines that further develop the imagery and usually introduce a lyrical, subjective element. In most cases, the three-line unit could stand alone as a haiku, while the next two-line unit is dependent on the other for its meaning and content."

Here is an example written by McClintock:

early snow . . .
from the islands of the north,
ice-packed bonito;
since summer I have waited
to hear the fish-monger's call!

The first three lines stand alone as a haiku and are modified by the last two lines. The third line, "ice-packed bonito," acts as a pivot line, making a haiku with both the first two or the last two lines.

Here is another of McClintock's taika. Again, his two lines of comments follow a haiku:

> leading my horse
> to the river at night
> scattered stars
> in such impossible numbers
> we don't mind drinking a few.

And here is the taika I quoted in the first chapter by Stephanie Bolster, where an original haiku is actually included:

> "my mini garden
> of crocuses and snowdrops
> tiny though lovely"
> first haiku I ever wrote
> now tanka of nostalgia

Just as witty haiku have a name of their own, *senryu*, so do witty tanka. They are called *kyōka* and are often parodies or satires. M. Kei calls them *anti-tanka*. I'll write more about them in a later chapter, but note them here as a variety of tanka.

I will also discuss tanka as ekphrastic poems in a later chapter, but I'd like to mention here the use of tanka as a diary form. I have complained elsewhere about tanka magazines reading like the trivia of everyday experiences. Still, I do recognize that recording the everyday by writing tanka is a wonderful practice that can only sharpen your tanka sensibilities. Here is a famous tanka by Takuboku that I quoted earlier, about an event revealing a very personal moment of how he faced what was to be a very early death — a diary tanka, but far from trivial:

> wrote GREAT
> in the sand
> a hundred times
> forgot about dying
> and went on home

Actually, the mundane recording of daily events is the more likely way tanka are written in Japan today, whereas writers in English tend to want to be profound or want the event recorded to be a special moment. Of his daily tanka writing, Sanford Goldstein wrote: "Poetry must not be what is usually called poetry. It must be an exact report, an honest diary of the changes in a man's emotional life."

Makoto Ōka clearly defines the diary-like quality of many tanka written in Japanese: "While haiku can be called the crystallization of fugitive instants, one might call waka or tanka the endless stream of sentiments and thoughts experienced in daily life."

I gave an example of minimal tanka earlier. Minimal tanka seem to have a growing group of aficionados, although some poets question whether the form isn't just a stretched haiku. Here is another by Michael McClintock:

> the recluse
> opens
> the door
> only for
> his cat

and one by Sanford Goldstein:

> downtown
> I pass
> something —
> humanity
> on a stoop

Whether you are writing a tanka string, tanka prose, trying a witty tanka, or using a tanka to mourn a departed friend, whatever form your tanka writing takes, it can be just the right size to express your every thought and emotion.

LOVE TANKA

when you opened
my letter
were you surprised
my heart
fell out?

    – Michael McClintock

IMAGINE THAT YOU LIVE MOST OF YOUR LIFE IN DARKENED
rooms, hidden behind screens, and swathed in many layers
of clothing. Your serving women shield you from intruders
. . . but not always. The full moon can be seen through the
shutters, and the sound of a nearby carriage can be heard.
A door slides open and closes, and suddenly your room is
pervaded by some wondrous smell. Cedar? Sandalwood?
Before you know it a man's voice is speaking softly to you,
and your layers of clothing are being separated. No use
in struggling, for this is fate. He stays with you all night
and then leaves reluctantly at the first light of day. No use
in crying at the damage done either, for soon you will be
receiving a flowering branch with a note attached to it. The
note is a tanka telling of how the man longs to see you again
and of the glories of your long black hair. You will need your
wits about you, even after a night of gymnastics, to respond
with a similar tanka reflecting, maybe more obliquely, on the
possibilities of continued meetings.

We are speaking of tanka here, for tanka was the language

of lovers as well as of seducers and those seduced. If the seduced woman responded with a touching, witty, and elegant tanka, she could depend on her lover not only returning, but possibly supporting her for the rest of her life. A good tanka had that much power. As the courtiers didn't go to war, or even hunt, what was left but love affairs . . . and tanka-writing?

Here is a series of tanka parodying a possible sequence of events for a court romance. It possibly started gently with a mildly flirtatious tanka of inquiry such as this:

> I hear
> a beauteous flower
> lives within
> this neglected garden
> would I could tend it

If the sender was high-ranking at court, the woman's servants would encourage her to reply, even if she was reluctant. Half a dozen such to and fro tanka, and the result was much like the seduction first described. Of course the male servant delivering the *billet-doux* would flirt with the woman's servants, and love (or sexual vibes) would be flowing all around.

If the man does not follow up regularly after the first visit, he might receive a long series of reproachful tanka from the woman, along the lines:

you said
you would tend
this neglected flower
how she withers away
longing for your touch

This does not encourage him, and when he does write, he makes loads of excuses . . . all in tanka form, of course:

the path
to the neglected flower
has been forbidden me
these last few months
oh woe is me!

We (and she) know he doesn't mean it. If, on the other hand, the courtship progresses well, her lover may consider having a new wing built on his house so as to cover her damaged reputation. Genji, the hero of *The Tale of Genji*, had so many women installed in his house that it must have looked like a rabbit's warren.

The wife in these situations, if there was one, would not be happily tolerating all these comings and goings and might well choose to retreat to her parent's house, albeit leaving a terse little tanka behind:

your gathering
of all these neglected flowers
untidies the place
if you do not sort this out
your lead blossom will be leaving

Of course, all these tanka, loving or not loving, would be filled with clever puns and alliterations, even though tempers might be high, for an elegant person would be beholden to write a good tanka about the situation, no matter what.

Some Heian Court women, such as Sei Shonagon and Izumi Shikibu, were independent and chose their lovers as they willed, though they too would do it all through tanka messages. Tanka truly is the poetry of seduction, of love, of longing. The Heian period in Japan was one where poetry and sex went hand in hand. Would that our age be as eloquent about the matter.

In a more serious vein, love as expressed in tanka, can also include all kinds of desire and the reflection of the futility and suffering that desire causes. Tanka writers in English, particularly those who move to tanka after writing haiku, welcome the ability to tell the reader directly of their requited or unrequited love and the impossibility of it all.

when I am gone
doctors will donate this heart
to someone else
only to find you
deep within the scar tissue

    — Kathy Lippard Cobb

set on my path,
I wasn't expecting
that kiss
sweeping away
all my maps

    — Jan Foster

Young love in memory:

we meet again
after fifty-two years . . .
my teen lover
you were so much taller
in my mind's eye

    — Amelia Fielden

And another by Fielden of love settled way down:

> *Russian ballet*
> *the elaborate sets*
> *the great leaps . . .*
> *now to catch the bus home*
> *to "what's for dinner?"*

You don't have to fall in or out of love in order to write brilliant tanka, but you do have to feel passionately and deeply about whatever you are writing.

NOSTALGIA AND TANKA

an old photo
of my parents
young and happy —
of all the things I own
that is the saddest

    — Michael McClintock

I've this memory —
riding my father's shoulders
into the ocean,
the poetry of things
before I could speak

    — Michael McClintock

As ONE AGES, EVERY NEW FACE SEEMS TO BE A REMINDER of a past face, and every object seems to send out memory waves. For me, tanka is the perfect vehicle for present regrets of past commissions and omissions and for the sadness that all things must pass. Often tanka seem to me to be like early photos, sepia-colored and full of memories.

Amelia Fielden and Sanford Goldstein are masters of nostalgia tanka, not just because they have years behind them, but because the past always seems to be trailing their tanka even when their tanka seem to be only of the present.

I put
long-ago desire
in a tin box
its tight tarnished lid
too hard to force open

    – Sanford Goldstein

two careers
three dogs, five children . . .
those were the days
when the clock panted
to keep up with us

    – Amelia Fielden

hilly paths
I walk where
once I ran . . .
sometimes the past
must be enough

    – Amelia Fielden

ripeness is all . . .
perhaps so for peaches, but
ah! those green years
experimenting
careless of time's steady tread

    – Amelia Fielden

all those good years
of family, life, friends, work
travel —
what if I lose the key
to my memories now

    – Amelia Fielden

And here are a few nostalgic tanka from other writers:

leaves ripple
on a reflecting pool
as autumn ends —
the life we remembered
is not the one we lived

    – John Martell

a sea breeze
and salt air left behind
on moving day
memories like grains of sand
stuck between my toes

    – Susan Constable

in a velvet box
her strand of pearls
still broken
a promise he made
when they were young

    – Susan Constable

he flies off
leaving behind
the cans and boxes
of a past life, and maybe one person
to trace his journey on a torn map

    – Naomi Beth Wakan

poets gather
under the plum tree
shadows on the page . . .
aren't all our ventures
tinged by the past?

    – Naomi Beth Wakan

And here is Tom Clausen's tanka that I quoted in the first chapter, but it is so cleverly nostalgic that it deserves to be requoted here:

wanting my old life
when I wanted
my present life
stirring the soup she made
as a cold rain falls outside

Being a land of immigrants, nostalgia in North America
sometimes takes the form of longing for one's homeland or
what one would like one's homeland to be:

longing
for a village with
thatched roofs . . .
a village I remember
only through books

    – Naomi Beth Wakan

longing always
for a home, that even
when I have one
I still feel myself
with a residual longing

    – Naomi Beth Wakan

Here is a beautiful love tanka also full of nostalgia:

> watching her sweep up
> November's fallen leaves
> I am love shaken . . .
> her body moving almost
> as it did when we were young
>
> — George Knox

Of course, these tanka examples go deeper than nostalgia, which often is just a kind of neurotic clinging to an imaginary past. The most interesting tanka often seek to link us to our past in order to reassure us of our present.

WITTY TANKA — KYŌKA

M. KEI, THE SOUL BEHIND *Atlas Poetica*, A JOURNAL OF world tanka, complains that tanka in English are very mannered with their "first half natural image, second half an emotional situation." He calls them "American Mannerism — Japanese tanka in a coonskin cap." Not all tanka written in English are done in the form he describes — that of a haiku plus two lines — but I do appreciate his criticism. Many tanka in English also seem very stilted to me, as if the writer is just imitating the waka of a thousand years ago. A few of them, however, break my heart with their integrity.

When I began to seek out witty tanka written in English, I too found them in the minority. M. Kei defines the duties of *kyōka*, the name for traditional witty thirty-one-syllable poetry, as "to point out muzzy-headed thinking, unexamined assumptions, and ill-conceived ideas." He also feels that when written in English, kyōka should be able to include "the tasteless, the juvenile and yes, even rhyme," as they did in Japanese. M. Kei finds that being able to write about taboo subjects is another reason to write kyōka. He claims that moving from the usual topics of thwarted love and the ephemeralness of living to more intimate, challenging, and forbidden topics brings fresh vitality to one's tanka writing, and I'm sure he is correct. Kei has also noted that many tanka journals would not accept his "witty" tanka, finding them too juvenile or bawdy. (I had a similar experience when an interesting tanka of mine was criticized because the topic was picking one's nose.) By defining them as a separate form of poetry rather than a sub-genre of tanka, M. Kei allows a space for a more relaxed five-line form of poetry. Some people feel it is totally unnecessary to use the word kyōka and have a separate category for such poetry, since they feel that witticisms, satire, and parody are quite common in tanka written in English.

I look for amusement, or at least some degree of cynicism, in my tanka. Whether or not the tanka shocks with its satire and subject seems irrelevant to me and really depends on the shockability of the reader. The interesting thing for me is that witty tanka, like *senryu* in haiku, conceal so much wisdom within their wittiness; at least the best of them do. I'll illustrate with a few. Here are a couple by Audrey Olberg, the first I quoted earlier:

> *Christmas carols*
> *on the radio —*
> *my aunt Ida Rose*
> *sings along*
> *in Yiddish*

and

> *winter lovemaking —*
> *socks*
> *booties*
> *a flannel nightie*
> *somehow he manages*

The first presents the isolation that minority groups experience at times when the majority of their neighbors are celebrating something outside their culture. In a joyful and incongruous way, Aunt Ida is breaching the gap, as Jews have so often converted suffering to humor over their many years of persecution. One wonders if Aunt Ida is doing a direct translation from the English, or whether she is making up her own words to familiar music. Either way, the image is strong and beautifully funny. It is not a racist tanka, or a put down of Aunt Ida's possible inability to speak the dominant language, English. It is a joyous accounting of a cross-cultural moment. In Olberg's second tanka, one hears echoes of the many-layered gowns of the Heian Court women as they are being seduced. It is a wonderful take-off of those moments so clearly recorded in Heian Court diaries when the man forces his way into the darkened room and works his way through the layers of clothes in order to complete the seduction. Instead of robes, we have the ways of keeping warm in bed in a cold climate — booties, socks, and flannel nighties. I'm surprised a hot water bottle wasn't introduced. The image is strong, the sentiment is very human, and the whole thing made me laugh out loud, which few regular tanka do.

I have checked out a number of kyōka on M. Kei's site and must admit that I'm a little too Puritan to be as playful as he is with my tanka writing. Genitals and bodily functions can be the focus of witty tanka, as anything else can, but, like love tanka, sometimes enough is enough. Still, I can see his point about liberating that way of writing tanka, and I admire his braveness at writing kyōka that he knows few tanka journals would accept. His kyōka may lead to a new way of writing witty tanka, or they may not. I feel that too much dwelling on farts, body parts, and bodily functions may indicate anxiety rather than genuine wit. By the way, I should remind you again that M. Kei does not even count kyōka as a tanka subset, but as a form that can almost be entitled "anti-tanka" in that they are a protest at tanka's formalism.

Here is one of M.Kei's more frivolous efforts:

> if I sit here
> listening to your poetry
> very much longer
> I will be wrinkled
> like an old woman

I'd like to finish my examples with a witty tanka by Sonja Arntzen, who, as a translator of Heian diaries — the *Kagero Diary* and the *Sarashina Diary* — is deeply immersed in traditional tanka, yet has the quick wit to observe a clever juxtaposition in the here and now:

> "Poet's Cove"
> declares the resort's
> splendid sign —
> on the chart it is right
> next to Starvation Bay

I appreciate exactly what she is able to connect in a real-life sailing situation. She saw the two names and wittily joined them without telling us why. Starving poets may be a cliché, but clichés are ways of expressing the familiar. Most of us don't like straying too far from the familiar, but, as here, enjoy a fresh connection. My own tanka below could almost be a response kyōka to that of Arntzen's:

> at the bank
> the teller discusses
> lay-offs
> I'm secure in the thought
> "I live by my poetry"

If you would like to know more about traditional kyōka writing in Japan, you could not do better than peruse Robin Gill's enormous tome, *Mad in Translation: A Thousand Years of Kyōka*. In the beginning, Gill announces that it is impossible to translate these kyōka because of the many puns and then proceeds to do just that for 740 pages. This is an extraordinarily detailed, academic, yet witty account of one thousand years of bawdy, outrageous, satirical, parody tanka. It can be read online. Wonderful examples of modern day kyōka can be found in the laugh-out-loud magazine, *Prune Juice*.

Shiki pronounced that "he who appreciates serious literature but not the comic should discuss neither." I feel that way about folks who treat haiku and tanka seriously, yet ignore senryu and kyōka as lesser forms of poetic expression. As a promoter of the wise clown, I beg you to try a few kyōka yourselves and see if you just don't reveal a few more deeper truths in that way of communicating than in your possibly more straightforward way of telling things as you see them.

To end this chapter, some examples to leave you at least smiling:

> I don't live alone
> I have a roommate named
> "Poverty"
> if only he would get married
> and move out!
>   – M. Kei

> when bankers
> jumped out
> of windows —
> those were the good
> old days
>   – Michael McClintock

> people rushing
> to and fro,
> something has to
> occupy their minds
> but what?
>   – M. Kei

I invite him
to join me
in my double kayak —
next day he telephones
asks to borrow it

   – Peggy Heinrich

two months
I wait to hear
from him
then a card
with my name spelled wrong

   – Angela Leuck

feeling uneasy
and walking faster
past the cardboard sign
taped to a tree —
"Pit Bulls 4 Sale"

   – Michael McClintock

The holiday season begins
early this year
as my family keeps pushing
my buttons as if
I were a vending machine

   – Alexis Rotella

a three week wait
and a four mile walk
to watch
my doctor
Google my symptoms

    – Liam Wilkinson

we never go
to sleep on an argument . . .
our custom's to kiss
then spend the night fighting
over the bedcovers

    – Claire Everett

RESPONSE TANKA

I FIRST MET SONJA ARNTZEN, THE SCHOLAR OF CLASSICAL
Japanese literature, when she came to one of my writing
workshops. Perhaps she was hoping to wean from
her academic style that had been necessary during her
professorial career. Soon we became friends, and she spoke
often to me about tanka, it being embedded within the diary
translations she was working on. I had heard of tanka before
but was reluctant to try it. Once started, however, I melted
into its stream as if I had always been a natural tanka writer.
As we both wrote, stimulated by sending tanka back and
forth, it was as if Arntzen and I had recaptured together
something of the tanka writing between friends at the Heian
Court and later. Out of this tanka friendship came two
books of response tanka, *Double Take* and *Reflections*.

Jan Foster, who wrote response tanka with her poet friend,
Amelia Fielden, says this about what she calls "responsive
tanka": "Here was the age-old form of letter writing, a
communication between friends, but in a delightfully
different style. Considering the thoughts of another person
and replying to them, but carrying the conversation into
a new direction, brought an added spice to the process
of composing tanka." Fielden has guided so many of her
tanka-writing friends towards responsive tanka and has
many books out on this form of tanka.

Here's a section entitled "Travel" from Arntzen and my
to-and-fro tanka that is in *Reflections*. This part was
using **utamakura**, for which Arntzen gave the following

introduction: "'Travel' was a frequent category in classical anthologies of Japanese waka. A concept connected with travel poems, though not limited to them, was **utamakura** or 'poem pillow.' The idea was that certain place names had a powerful resonance — usually acquired from their presence in poems of the past — that made them natural pillows or supports for new poems. In Japanese, these place names were often five or seven syllable units, which means they could provide the poet one whole line already freighted with a constellation of associations. There are really no place names in modern English with the same kind of richness in shared meaning. Within this next section of poems about travel, however, we have tried to use place names that most people will know."

Wakan —

> once shaken loose
> from your homeland
> any spot
> on this dusty road
> can seem like home

Arntzen —

> oh, to be cut loose
> from this worrying mind
> that finds no solace
> anywhere, can't even
> imagine the feeling of home

Wakan —

> it was in Istanbul
> that we drew east and west
> together
> as we crossed the Bosphorus
> sharing a coat against the cold

Arntzen —	flying to Tokyo
	for the first time . . . I crossed the
	international date line
	that holds time apart
	on the sea's trackless unity

Wakan —	my memories
	of London are closer
	to Dickens
	with his twisted streets and hearts
	than what it possibly is now

Arntzen —	even underfoot
	the real streets of London
	seem more
	like stage sets for films
	of Sherlock Holmes and Poirot

Response tanka depend so much on the two poets being on the same page, as it were, and Arntzen and I certainly were. Sometime later, however, I did a successful book of response tanka with someone completely different from me, both in life and on the written page. David Bateman is a gay, academic, city-dwelling poet, and I am sunk in domesticity in the country. Bateman crams his tanka with metaphor, so I had to dive deep to see what he was up to in order to respond. Here are a couple of response tanka from our book:

Prologue

Bateman —

she writes lives clearly
daily sculpting joy with woe
excess lines shed
while he furnishes castles
with moth filled lacy language

Wakan —

he writes
of worlds unimagined
within her brackets . . .
of costume parties where
the masked are never unmasked

Epilogue

Bateman —

weaving gentle ties
she threads lithe and subtle strands
into pleasured land
through verses wrought with wisdom
word garments sheathed in loving

Wakan —

her world is small
immediate to the point of petty
his horizons are at
the outer edges of the universe
occasionally they lean together

Next is a wonderful set of response tanka that very much appeals to my domestic slant on life:

For Good Measure

> by Autumn Noelle Hall and Claire Everett

on the sill, Ball jars
empty of all but sea-green
sunlight . . .
her memories of canning
slipping, like skin from a peach

damsons
blush-indigo to damask
gems from bough to jar
gifts from the Romans
to my mother, to me

bumblebee-dizzy
on fermented fruit perfume
she giggles
spreading pinafore to catch
what brother shakes from the tree

a fluted edge
and an apple pie smile
patting and pricking
I make-believe the trimmings
into something warm and sweet

tin cutters:
hearts, stars, gingerbread men
pressed into scraps
the way those days were shaped
and sugar-sprinkled

not quite big enough
each spoonful of her not quite
sweet enough jam
like a small surgeon, I watch,
be-gloved with shortcrust dough

upside-down in the
bowl of her silver teaspoon,
faces, time-tarnished
loosened wisps of hair curled
against steam-ruddied cheeks

down three steps
to the fragrant, red tiled chill
of Grandma's pantry –
the love she could not show us
melted in our mouths

stuck to cellar shelves
green tomato marmalade
wreathed in cobwebs
her need to preserve even
labor's unripe fruits

chopping mint
with a curved blade —
sickle moon,
all that she kept concealed
expressed in the details

on her hands
as on her old butcher block
visible scars
some pits resist removal
some stones cling to flesh

holding my breath
I remove the spine intact.
how weak this flesh
clinging to promises
just as easily broken

hogs head cheese
bits of brain and cheek meat jelled
in its own aspic
having to make do with scraps
learning to stomach this . . .

leftovers
simmering on the stove
this thin broth
fragrant with thyme, enough
to fill memory's childhood home

the scent of bread
rising from the oven's warmth
fills the emptiness
all the little tricks she had
for leavening our lives

deep in the core
brown sugar, fruit and spices
fit to burst
slow-baking Bramley apples
while you tell me all your plans

leaving at first light
the kettle cold on the stove
you take only
your favorite wooden spoon
to stir up a whole new life

safely gathered in
"may you never hunger,
may you never thirst . . ."
how the years come and go
measured by place-settings

Sonja Arntzen wrote the following great introduction for
our book of response tanka, *Double Take,* and I think it may
help readers understand the process of writing response
tanka, so I am including it here: "For many years, as part of
teaching courses on classical Japanese literature, I created
and participated in exercises where the students and I
would write poems in English but in Japanese forms like

haiku and tanka as a way to deepen our appreciation of Japanese poetry. It was only after coming to live on Gabriola Island that I shifted toward writing tanka as means of expressing my experience for its own sake. One catalyst was subscribing to a fledgling tanka journal, *Gusts*, that was started by a friend, Kozue Uzawa, which provided a venue for tanka submissions. The other catalyst was becoming friends with Naomi Wakan, the well-known haiku poet and inspired provocateur of writing in others. Naomi involved me in workshops, where she taught haiku and I taught tanka. Naomi herself took up the tanka form enthusiastically. Just last year, Naomi acquired a book of tanka poetry written by two Australian poets, Amelia Fielden and Kathy Kituai entitled *In Two Minds*, a book of what they called 'responsive tanka.' To have two short poems create a conversation with each other brought a whole new dimension into the presentation of tanka in English. Reading the book with delight, I mentioned to Naomi that we could try exchanging tanka for fun. 'We certainly could and we'll make a book out of it!' was her response. Before I knew it, she had the book all planned out. Naomi is the only person I know who considers the writing of poetry seriously as a livelihood. And thus, this book was born.

"Now, the idea of using tanka as a media for give-and-take communication is not new. There is an old Chinese adage, 'Warm up the old to know the new' and it is surely true in this case. Tanka have been written in Japan since the 7th century and during most of that long history, tanka were exchanged in written and spoken communication. To be correct, prior to the modern period, this form of poetry was known as waka. Waka and tanka are, however, exactly the same in form. Tanka is the ancestor of haiku which only came into being in the 17th century. Haiku can be described as the beginning of a tanka left open to be completed in the reader's mind. One of the interesting aspects of Japanese literary history is this gradual movement toward forms of greater and greater compression. I would suggest one reason why short forms have had such a long life in Japan was the role they played in communication. If most members of society are going to compose poetry for impromptu exchange in day to day communication, it is simply better if the poems are short.

"Haiku, as a poetic form, has been enthusiastically adopted into the English language, and indeed many other languages in the world. Tanka has a smaller following but seems to be increasing its practitioner base. Generally, composers of haiku and tanka in English ignore most of the prosodic conventions in the Japanese poetic tradition. The bare minimum definition of the two forms is that tanka is a five line poem and haiku is three line poem. If one has confined oneself to writing haiku for a long time, those extra two lines in tanka can feel, as Naomi so disarmingly puts it, that one has been given 'total freedom.' Suddenly there is room for the overt expression of feeling, and such luxuries as similes and metaphors.

"Although Japanese tanka is the source for the form of poetry we have written in this work, [*Double Take*] I do not think these tanka are written in a 'Japanese way.' When we assembled the poems, however, I witnessed the coming into play of linking dynamics that I have enjoyed in Japanese poetry. In the Japanese poetic tradition, poems have not been thought of as having 'fixed' meanings. Compilers of anthologies have always been aware that a poem can mean one thing on its own and then something quite different when juxtaposed with another poem. I felt this vividly as I looked for already written poems to match with poems of Naomi's and when I was writing new poems as a direct response to hers. One instance that provided great pleasure was the response to Naomi's poem about living by her poetry:

> at the bank
> the teller discusses
> lay-offs
> I'm secure in the thought
> "I live by my poetry"

"What came to me was an experience of the previous spring that had not yet crystallized into a poem. I lay ill in bed a lot of last May. The forced leisure gave me the opportunity to listen to the song sparrows' melodious calls to the point that I could recognize the individual singers and almost score their tunes. One day I got to see one of these reclusive birds on the fence outside our window and watch how his whole body went into his song. The words fell into place to catch the wonder I felt at that moment.

a scrawny song sparrow
lifts up its throat, lets forth
trill after trill —
ruler of the world
reached by its song

"By itself, the tanka catches a moment of observed nature, but in juxtaposition with Naomi's poem, it becomes humorously metaphorical.

"Sometimes the link between the tanka is by a single word, sometimes by shared subject, imagery, or tone. Sometimes the link is close, other times it is distant. Always between the two poems there is a resonance that expands the meaning beyond the sum of the two separate poems."

EKPHRASTIC TANKA

EKPHRASIS ORIGINALLY MEANT THE DESCRIBING OF objects so clearly that the reader could easily picture them, even if they were imaginary. The word comes from the Greek *ekphrazein* — to recount, describe — from *ex*, meaning "out" and *phrazein*, meaning "to point out, explain."

Ekphrasis can also apply to any medium being used to describe and enhance another. When it comes to describing works of art, ekphrasis can include: (1) the writer speaking to the work of art; (2) the work of art speaking for itself; (3) the writer describing the work of art in detail; (4) the writer speaking of the ideas, emotions, and feelings that the work gives rise to; and (5) the writer speaking of the moment when the work is observed, that is, the work in its momentary setting.

Ekphrastic tanka can serve to enhance works of creativity. Once, I volunteered Susan Constable, Sonja Arntzen, and myself to the challenge of writing tanka or haiku to match forty-five photographs displayed by a Central Vancouver Island photography club. It took us four hours to match words to photographs. We were justifiably triumphant at the end of the long session.

Ekphrastic tanka not only serve to enrich the work, but can also just describe it and stand as tanka in their own right. Of the examples below, the first four are mine.

The following tanka was inspired by *The Gleaners* by Jean-François Millet, 1857. Oil on canvas. (In the collection of the Musée d'Orsay in Paris, France, and may be seen on its website.)

the scraps
the leftovers that
have to be stooped for
still can suffice if
one has modest demands

Homage to the Square: Aurora by Josef Albers, 1951-55. Oil on masonite. (In the collection of the Kemper Art Museum at Washington University in St. Louis, Missouri, and may be seen on its website.)

to abstract the sunrise
just place a yellow square
within a grey square
within a blue square
the edges blurring

Untitled, Study for Composition VII, First Abstraction by Wassily Kandinsky, 1913. Watercolor. (In the collection of the Centre Pompidou in Paris, France, and may be seen on its website.)

a child's smudges with
the sophistication of placement
that only comes
with years of careful looking
years of slowly removing the subject

With Sloping Mast and Dipping Prow by Albert Ryder,
1980-85. Oil on canvas. (In the collection of the Smithsonian
American Art Museum in Washington, DC, and may be seen
on its website.) Ryder was notorious for mixing various
paints together whether the medium mixed or not, so many
of his paintings are badly cracked and flaked.

a reminder
of the preciousness
of life
the fragile sailors clinging
to a fragile canvas

Here is Terry Ann Carter's sensitive tanka on a pieta:

this Pieta
by the seaside
a mother lifts her son
from his wheelchair
to sit by the water

Here is Jim Kacian's tanka on one of Joseph Beuys' "Stag" works:

> penciled in
> the shape of antlers
> that will be
> halfway between
> gods and men

These ekphrastic tanka by Janet Vicker are on paintings by Mindy Joseph. (See these works at www.mindyjoseph.com)

Purple Haze

> embedded in purple
> bleeding magenta
> an old man's face
> white and distorted
> fades

Aquagain

> among the blue-green tides
> and purple falls
> faces of those who drowned
> mouths and eyes open
> in awe

Wings

unfold from a dark center
out beyond form
they create a storm
colors choreograph
their ancestral dance

Emily Carr's paintings are a frequent source for ekphrastic inspiration. Here is a tanka by Leanne McIntosh on *Scorned as Timber, Beloved of the Sky*, 1935. Oil on canvas. (In the collection of the Vancouver Art Gallery in Vancouver, British Columbia, Canada, and may be seen on its website.)

the sky
rolling across earth
gathers me
into the calling of trees
into raven, eagle, thunderbird

The next tanka by Elehna de Sousa offers a general take on Emily Carr's works, many of which are in the collection of the Vancouver Art Gallery in Vancouver, British Columbia, Canada, and may be seen on its website.

Raven
with my paintbrush
spiralling
up and up . . .
through all these shades of green

Susan Constable's tanka, below, was inspired by *Lane in Normandy* by Claude Monet, 1868. Oil on canvas. (In the collection of Matsuoka Museum of Art, Tokyo, Japan, and may be seen on its website.)

heading home
this autumn evening
lamplight
through a bedroom window —
you, in the corner of my mind

Here is another tanka by Constable, inspired by William Brody's painting *A Place to Sit*:

this morning at ten:
the aroma of fresh bread
two cups of tea
the sound of your voice
when you say my name

Amelia Fielden has an interesting ekphrastic tanka inspired by Ichiryusai Hiroshige's *Rough Sea at the Naruto in Awa Province, no. 55*, 1855. Woodblock print on paper. (In the collection of The Gibbes Museum of Art, Charleston, South Carolina, and may be seen on its website.)

> white tentacles
> of foam frothing up
> from whirlpools
> in Prussian-blue sea,
> overpowering the rocks

John Martell offers the following tanka inspired by a painting by Ito Shinsui called *Eyebrow Pencil*, 1928. Color woodblock print. (In the collection of the Art Institute of Chicago, Chicago, Illinois, and may be seen on its website.)

> sending off
> a poem to her lover
> she uses
> the writing brush
> to darken her eyebrows

Tanka on Edward Hopper Paintings

Cape Cod Morning

looking
out the window
expecting
a bright new day
sharp shadows on the clapboard

City Roots

chimneys
as far as one
can see
and dirty skylights
letting in the city sky

New York Movie

the usherette
has seen the movie
a hundred times
lost in thought
she muses on her own drama

Nighthawks

the man behind
the counter is beaked
like a nighthawk
the customers sit in loneliness
even the couple

Room by the Sea

are the waters
always cerulean blue
and the woodwork
weathered over the years,
is it always ash grey?

TANKA AS SELF-EXPRESSION

wimpish
hiding under my narrow bed
from boyhood fears
wimpish as a man
upholding no cause

    – Sanford Goldstein

PROFESSOR SANFORD GOLDSTEIN, THE GODFATHER OF
tanka written in English, is also the master of self-confession,
as you can see in the above poem. Because of his many
translations of Japanese tanka, his tanka, in English, seem
imbued with the Japanese spirit. He writes up to twenty
tanka each day and has done so for years. These tanka
almost act as a diary. Of his copious output, Goldstein has
written, "I have been on my tanka road for more than fifty
years, so my eye has steadily been on tanka. That means of
course that I write about myself, the thoughts and feelings I
have, the people I meet, the images in front of me, the family
or relatives or a few lifelong friends. The possibilities are
immense."

As a personal essayist, I know the danger of recording one's
life as one is living it. I often ponder whether this doesn't
reduce the intensity of living, drain it off in words as it were.
On the other hand, it's possible that it allows poets and
personal essayists to maybe live life twice: once in reality
and once again in reflections.

Here is another one of Sanford's tanka that shows the openness and revealing style of his work:

half a tanka
will probably suffice
to say
this blur on life's page
is ready for erasure

Here is one of mine, written on demand, having been given the words "determination" and "family" to work into a poem in a kind of spontaneous challenge:

determination
never my strong point
for as a mother
I sometimes clung to family
sometimes packed my bags and ran

I was surprised at what came out, but then, that is the way with tanka writing, one is often surprised in this way.

As many tanka read like diaries covering day-to-day trivia and insights, they are the perfect poetry style to release our true voices and real feelings. Takuboku expresses for all of us the person inside who needs to be allowed a voice:

the trouble is
every man
keeps a prisoner
groaning
in his heart

Amelia Fielden is known for her devastatingly truthful tanka about her life, as in this example:

books, books, more books
"why do you read so much," asks
my husband
"our life's not enough for you?"
must I reply with the truth

Most tanka are written in the first person, and so it is natural that the ideas and feelings expressed will, to some extent, be self-revelatory. Writing tanka can't help but make you more aware of yourself, your feelings, and your motivations. I've found it a perfect outlet for frustrations and also for joy.

Family tanka

the relief
of acknowledging
I'm not
the genius my mother
thought I was

my mother
sat by the fire removing
psoriasis scales
the smell of singed chicken
and I'm back there with her

two young girls
arms scratched with brambles
seated side-by-side
on father's crazy-pavement doorstep
made for just such wild women

and through the mirror
at the end of the bed she sees
her baby's head crowning
and quickly prays for its future
in this world of foolishness

a nearly perfect rose
for my nearly perfect arrangement
to accompany
a nearly perfect meal, at which
my husband sits reading at the table

the eighteen-month
goes tippy-toe to view
his new sister
his brows wrinkle in confusion
at what her arrival might mean

the photo is faded
but how can I forget
his small face
looking so trustingly
up to my own

seeing
parents with children
I breathe in guilt . . .
not that I didn't want to be a mother,
just not to be one every day

the afternoon couch
the perfect place to hate
one's parents
dredge up the past and
blame it on someone

the first time
my two small children
spoke to each other
without me being needed . . .
a startling moment

TAN RENGA

When writing tanka, though there may be a
division between the first three lines and the last two either
in theme or tone, the whole five lines are written by one
person. In *tan renga*, the first three lines are written by
one person and then another poet completes the tanka. It
is interesting to see what twists and turns the second poet
makes to match and deepen the topic presented in the first
three lines. Of course, the first poet can present two lines
and have the second poet complete the remaining three.

The tan renga is really a short renga. You will remember that
I have already mentioned that haiku are derived from renga,
being the initial three lines of a renga session. So tan renga is
really one poet presenting a haiku and the second capping it
off with two lines.

Michael Dylan Welch gives two interesting examples of tan
renga in his article on the subject:

Carol Purington   small clouds
                                in a clear sky—also swallows
                                flying high
Larry Kimmel   all that I did today I did
                                as if her eyes were on me

Paul O. Williams	morning sun —
	all the patio tables
	shining with new rain
Michael Dylan Welch	church bells
	church bells

It is interesting to take a famous haiku and add your own two lines as I did with this haiku by Issa:

Issa	carrying his mother
	and leading his child by the hand
	cherry blossom
Wakan	burdens when accepted change
	to rose petals falling lightly

Here are a couple by two well-known tan renga writers, Kathe Palka and Peter Newton, co-editors of the website *Tiny Words*:

Palka	April darkness
	a tinge of green to the clouds
	as sirens whine
Newton	the poppy about to
	burst

Palka   *dining al fresco*

                        dogs and their owners

                        introduce each other

Newton   *that rain, she says*

                        was biblical

I often use tan renga when introducing students to tanka writing because writing five lines straight off is usually too demanding for non-poets. By offering them the first three lines and discussing them in detail, the students usually find it is simple to express what they feel or think about them in the remaining two lines.

JAPANESE SENSITIVITIES

all this talk
of what's a haiku?
what's a tanka?
oh, you short-poem enthusiasts
what's wabi? what's sabi?

    – Sanford Goldstein

WHEN I READ BOOKS ABOUT WRITING TANKA IN preparation for this book, I came up with no rules and no guidelines. It seems that the theme and the tone are the defining characteristics of tanka. As to what a tanka actually is, my only clue came to me through the reading of tanka . . . and yet more tanka . . . until I could only gasp and cry, "Yes" when I recognized a fine tanka. But I couldn't analyze it; I just knew.

When you are starting out in tanka, my advice is to read as many tanka as you can. You will find that understanding comes by osmosis or intuition. The tanka that resonate with you will be the kind of tanka you want to write, and writing them will allow you to break through your isolation into a sharing, a sharing of pains, sorrows, joys and triumphs.

Still, there are some qualities in Japanese culture that are useful to think about when you are writing tanka. These qualities usually speak to the tone of a poem, and I frequently try to explain that tone is what makes a tanka a tanka. In English, we don't have a word for a snowfall just heavy enough to make branches sag a little, as the Japanese do. Our language does not allow for such subtleties.

It also appears that Japanese poets have certain sensitivities that other poets find hard to duplicate, that is, according to Daisetz Suzuki. He speaks about such qualities as *wabi, sabi, yūgen, aware, shibui, hon-i, yojō, en, yushin*, and *makoto*. I'm not denying that these qualities find full development in Japanese poetry. Eric Sherlock explains, "This insularity (of Japan) allowed for the growth of a particularly unified aesthetic sensitivity that was to compensate for what the culture lacked in intellectual vigor." Even T. S. Eliot seemed in support of Suzuki when he stated, "No art form is more stubbornly national than poetry."

I, however, would like to plead the case that sensitivity to qualities such as awesomeness, ephemeralness, and spareness does not have national boundaries, and that any sensitive poet can express such qualities in their works. Poetry is a condensed form of human ideas and emotions. We are all human, so why can't non-Japanese poets express the qualities Suzuki listed above? I know little about these words so admired when exemplified in Japanese poetry and so decided to approach them from a strictly amateur point of view and see what I could discover about each and whether it would be possible for a non-Japanese person to appreciate them. In my naivety and lack of knowledge, I may misinterpret things, so please forgive me. However, I may also offer fresh ideas that make Japanese sensibilities into universal ones to which we, as poets, can all aspire. I write poetry as a practice perhaps towards enlightenment—though I have never found anyone able to precisely explain it, despite having traveled to distant lands and spoken with exotic lamas — or more practically and feasibly, towards being a more tolerable person to my husband, family, and friends. I hope these "Japanese" qualities are present in my writings in abundance and that they will fill your tanka too.

Let's begin with *wabi-sabi*, perhaps the most important quality listed. Wabi–sabi is, I think, being poor in the best sense, that is, not being dependent on material things, power, and society's approval — for example, Thoreau's cabin. Wabi-sabi is not, however, a paean to poverty; there is nothing admirable about poverty. Wabi-sabi is about the paring down of things so that one dwells in the essential. Many Japanese poets longed for this state but were actually wealthy and from noble families, thus making such a realization very difficult. Wabi-sabi is not the display of brilliance or intellectual ability; it is the state of being gently content with observing nature. Wabi-sabi gives a hint of loneliness, not the negative kind, more like solitude that allows for contemplation away from society's demands and others' intellectualization. It also touches on the ephemeral as it admires things that have been worn and torn by life: the cracked pottery cup, the patina-ed metal, the much scarred wooden floor — flawed beauty as it were (*sabi* actually means "rusty"). A wabi-sabi sensibility sees the bittersweetness of all things, the beauty in imperfection. Wabi-sabi is the art of the monochrome. Koren states, "Wabi-sabi refers to the delicate balance between the pleasure we get from things and the pleasure we get from freedom from things."

Another quality very present in Japanese writing is *yūgen*, to me, the ability to see the universal and unchanging behind all sensory observations. It suggests glimpses of the eternal in an ever-changing world; the absolute within the relative world, as it were. Since this cannot be directly expressed, such things as misty scenes are metaphors for this quality. Yūgen implies a depth of understanding perhaps well put by the Japanese poet Chōmei: "Only when many ideas are compressed in one word, when without displaying it you exhaust your mind in all its depth and you imagine the imperceptible, when commonplace things are used to display beauty and in a style of naiveté an idea is developed to the limits, only then, when thinking does not lead anywhere and words are inadequate, should you express your feelings by this method." With yūgen you are conveying something that paradoxically cannot be conveyed in words.

Aware – mono no aware, literally the pathos of things. Here the writer shows, I consider, a sensitivity to things that stir the reader to sympathy. It implies having the ability to appreciate a deeper beauty, a beauty particularly shown when nature is connected to the ephemeralness of all things. Such awareness of beauty raises an elegant and sophisticated kind of sympathy.

The term, *yojō* expresses ideas arising from allusions to the past, a kind of lingering feeling, emotional reverberations. Michael Dylan Welch, in a lecture, once wrote the word "tundra" on the board as a possible one-word haiku. The reverberations from that one word were immense. Yojō are "Feelings that transcend the words," the ideas, emotions, and connections that come to one after looking at a great work of art or reading a poem that reaches beyond the personal and the particulars of the age in which they were produced.

Makoto is, as Eric Sherlock expresses it, "the single-minded devotion to the totality of the aesthetic experience." Makoto is what I call "integrity"; it is the idea that no contrivance comes between the poet and their experience, between the actor and the action. Makoto is the sincerity that absorbs both poet and object, rising above them both. A person with makoto approaches life with all their heart. Of course, if one can do this, one can experience the void, the infinity at the core of matter. There is nothing sophisticated about this ability; rather, it is childlike and in some way unadulterated but still accessible to all human beings, I would think.

Shibusa is the austere, the subdued. It is a combination of spontaneity and restraint. Garr Reynolds' seven aspects of Japanese aesthetics come to mind when I think of shibusa. His aspects are simplicity, asymmetry, subtlety, naturalness, austerity, freedom from formula, and tranquility. All these qualities paradoxically involve a certain refinement in the sense that all artificiality is removed. Jiro Harada says of shibusa, "It is the quality which is quiet and subdued. It is natural and has depth, but avoids being too apparent, or ostentatious. It is simple without being crude, austere without being severe. It is that refinement that gives spiritual joy." Are we looking at what might be called "good taste" here? But, as my daughter reminds me, when I say "good taste," I really mean "my taste."

Kokoro is the capacity for feeling into the innermost

nature of things at a level that binds all things together—the message not the medium. Teika expresses it this way, "Poetry is not an art which can be learned by looking afield or hearing afar; it is something that proceeds from the heart and is understood in the self."

These qualities seem to be planted in Japanese poets' genes, so natural it appears for their poetry to be imbued with them. Many Japanese writers have luckily been able to understand these very Japanese concepts, as in the following example:

"Haiku is inspired by an immediate resonance between an intuition within the poet and an evocative image." This quote is by Eric Sherlock and how it parallels Bashō, with his "go to the pine if you want to learn about the pine." Again Eric Sherlock: "The haiku does not need to be profound, because everything is profound." Surely this is as Zen as it gets. He might as well have substituted the word "tanka" for "haiku" here. Eric Sherlock must know something as his quote shows he fully exemplifies Bashō's advice "attain a high stage of enlightenment and return to the world of common men." He well exemplifies Bashō again when he advises "no subjective explanations just identification with the poetic subject." How this parallels Bashō's advice that not a hair's breath should be between the poet and the object he/she is writing about.

Ezra Pound also hinted at some of these Japanese subtleties when he wrote: "[An image] is that which presents an intellectual and emotional complex in an instant of time… It is the presentation of such a 'complex' instantaneously which gives that sudden liberation; that sense of freedom from time limits and space limits, that sense of sudden growth which we experience in the presence of the greatest works of art."

the dark green
of Japanese workers' clothes
sturdy cloth
I touch it and think
"this is just what is needed"

– Naomi Beth Wakan

TANKA POETS — MY TEACHERS

THERE ARE SO MANY POETS WHO HELPED ESTABLISH
tanka outside Japan. I would start with Sanford Goldstein.
Then, Donald Keene, Jane Hirshfield, Jane and Werner
Reichhold, Kenneth Rexroth, Stephan D. Carter Arthur
Waley, Michael Dylan Welch, Michael McClintock, Denis M.
Garrison, Dorothy Howard, Pamela Ness, Beverley George,
Kozue Uzawa, George Swede, and David Terelinck, to
name but a few. If you explored any of these poets' websites
and their writings, you would have a good foundation for
starting to write tanka yourself. The magazines that have
promoted tanka, such as *Blithe Spirit* (United Kingdom),
Kokako (New Zealand), *Red Lights* (USA), *Gusts* (Canada),
and *Eucalypt* (Australia), have also played an important
part.

I should also mention an indebtedness to translators such
as Arthur Waley, Stephan Carter, and Sanford Goldstein, but
here, however, I would just like to reminisce about the tanka
writers with whom I have had personal contact.

I cannot remember when I heard the word tanka for the very
first time. Long ago, I initiated an annual gathering of haiku
poets at our home on Gabriola Island, and some notable
poets attended every year. I remember them speaking of
renga and tanka, and both words felt vaguely familiar, but
I didn't take much interest as I was so absorbed in the
practice of writing haiku at the time.

It was some years into these gatherings that I realized I had already read a great deal of tanka in my perusal of Robert H. Brower and Earl Miner's book, *Japanese Court Poetry*, as well as in my annual reading of *Genji Monogatari*, the first novel ever written in the world. In the days when Murasaki Shikibu wrote *Genji*, tanka were known as waka, and she wrote 795 of them within the one thousand and more pages of that book. "So those are tanka," I remember saying to myself.

Sonja Arntzen, the scholar of classical Japanese literature, of whom I spoke earlier, just happens to live on the island where I live, Gabriola, and she offered to give a workshop on tanka, which I attended. I remember being frustrated and lost, for, as we've seen, tanka-writing has none of the clear rules of haiku-writing. "Why was it that the other students were 'getting it' and I wasn't?" I pondered. I took books on tanka out of the library, searching for what would guide me in writing this particular form of poetry, so tempting to me because it would seemingly allow me a lot of freedom that haiku, with its heavy expectations, didn't. I can't remember when things clicked into place, but click they did, and I was off and away with a vengeance.

In my pursuit of how to write tanka, I read work by early pioneers of tanka in English, such as Jane Reichold, Pamela Ness, Patricia Prime, Michael McClintock, and Alexis Rotella.

Sanford Goldstein, is perhaps the godfather of tanka writing in English. Sanford Goldstein was recognized as the English-language authority on tanka when he was chosen to be the first judge of the Mirrors First International Awards in 1989.

He has become a legend in his time for writing at least ten tanka every day. Of his writing of tanka, he said, "... in the 1960s, back in the States, I came across Carl Sesar's *Poems to Eat*, English translations of somebody called Takuboku. I felt like Keats on first looking into Chapman's Homer." Later he added, "I knew tanka was the form for me. I discovered that tanka was a vehicle through which I could endlessly talk about my life, my feelings, and my thoughts." That was something I was to feel myself.

Takuboku Ishikawa, whom Goldstein mentions as having a strong influence on him, was also a tanka writer who affected me through his poems translated by Carl Sesar.

I was lucky enough to meet up with Michael Dylan Welch when, for many years, he attended our annual haiku gathering on Gabriola. I was immediately impressed by his generous sharing of his immense knowledge, knowing nothing at that time of his influence in establishing the tanka form of poetry in North America. Welch's haiku and tanka achievements would run to several pages, since there is hardly any place in the haiku-tanka world of North America where his footprint can't be found. His essays on tanka on his website, www.graceguts.com, provide ample information on tanka and tanka writing for anyone wanting to try the form, and that included me. In 1994, Welch edited and published what was probably the first anthology of English-language tanka, titled *Footsteps in the Fog*. In 2000, he founded the Tanka Society of America (TSA) and served as the group's president for five years. He has judged and placed in numerous tanka contests, co-directed the 2003 TSA Tanka Day in New York City, and in 2003 edited the first TSA members' anthology, *Castles in the Sand*. Despite his many achievements and activities both in the haiku- and the tanka-writing worlds, he is generous with his time and seriously considers all questions put to him in the field of short-form Japanese poetry.

I met Amelia Fielden, one of the leading present-day translators of tanka and a wonderful tanka writer herself, when she visited Gabriola for one of the annual haiku weekends that I hosted. She is Australian, and a lot of her tanka reflect her appreciation of the local flora. She presented a lecture to the group gathered and introduced me to the idea of responsive tanka since she had, as I mentioned earlier, written several books with co-poets in which they alternated tanka to and fro as if corresponding with each other.

The first of the two response tanka books Sonja and I wrote, *Double Take*, was published by Modern English Tanka Press, which, at that time, was run by Denis Garrison. Garrison has worn many hats in a varied life: sailor, airman, mechanic, electrician, debt collector, sporting goods salesman, quality control technician, boiler-room operator, bureaucrat, small businessman, priest, poet, editor, and publisher. Together with Michael McClintock, Garrison edited the new wave tanka anthologies: *The Five-Hole Flute*, *The Dreaming Room*, *Landfall*, and *Streetlights*. It is as publisher that he influenced and supported my tanka writing and so many other tanka writers too.

As I started to enter the tanka world, I began to submit my first tentative efforts to such magazines as Beverley George's

Eucalypt, and Kozue Uzawa's *Gusts*. Beverley George is the foremost champion of haiku, tanka, and haibun in Australia, as is Patricia Prime in New Zealand. Kozue Uzawa, the editor of *Gusts*, a Canadian tanka journal, has also visited Gabriola. She translates Japanese tanka and co-published *Ferris Wheel: 101 Modern and Contemporary Tanka*, which received the 2007 Donald Keene Translation Award for Japanese Literature. I have had many tanka accepted by Kozue, and she has been so encouraging to the more than two hundred tanka writers who have appeared in the pages of her magazine.

In typical Japanese fashion, I bow very low to all those named above in gratitude for helping me on my tanka path.

ENVOI

IN MY BOOK *Poetry That Heals*, I SPEAK OF HOW LEARNING
to write tanka helped me get in touch with feelings that I
formerly had kept well under wraps. It also taught me to
accept that life is bittersweet and not to always yearn for
security and happiness. As if that isn't enough reward, I also,
over the years, have met so many good-willed poets who
helped me to go a little deeper into things than my usual
skimming-over-life self usually allowed. I have found only
generosity and support from the many haiku- and tanka-
writing poets who have come my way over the years. They
may split hairs as to whether a haiku is a haiku or a senryū,
or grumble at the lack of outlets where one can send one's
tanka efforts, but by and large, these are minor moments.
Sharing a sigh with them when a perfect tanka is read at a
gathering is a moment I cherish.

While haiku flood the web, tanka is less familiar. Because
tanka is less cocooned in rules, its development in the
world of non-Japanese poetry seems a little amorphous
and certainly open to many possibilities. Tanka, remains
my favorite form of poetry to write, and I will follow its
development closely. I do hope I have caught you up in my
tanka-world, if only for a brief moment.

Tidal pool tanka

tidal pools
sand ripples, water ripples,
sunlight ripples,
what a fine piece of weaving
this beach has produced

a hermit crab
drags its home on its back
the length of the pool
our mortgage paid
I have no such burden

tidal pool
the barnacles kick open
one by one
I know they are feeding
but somehow I feel welcomed

high tide
the tidal pool disappears
water over water . . .
lost in the day's news
I await the tide turning

TANKA EXERCISES

1. Read as many tanka as you can, feeling out the
    qualities that you think make a "good" tanka.

2. Try writing a tanka in which the first part is a question
    and the second part is the answer. For example:

    wind from the beach
    what does it foretell?
    the color of autumn
    and the falling away of desire
    as the maple keys fall

    – Naomi Beth Wakan

    our life in this world —
    to what shall I compare it?
    it is like a boat
    rowing out at break of day
    leaving not a trace behind

    – Somi Mansei

3. Focus on a sense image: something tactile, tasty, a smell,
    a sound, something you can see. Describe it in the first
    three lines (short, long, short). Then reflect on what you
    have written, and add the last two lines (long, long).

4. Now try the third exercise again for a fresh tanka and see if you can write a good pivot line — usually the third line.

5. Try writing a tanka with a different image on each line and yet make it a whole and cohesive poem.

6. The more tanka you write, the more likely you are to understand them. Try writing at least one tanka each day. It could act as a diary recording some event. You can date the tanka or add comments about the day. Looking back at the end of the year, you will probably find a good number that are worth a little editing to make them into interesting tanka.

SOURCES

Books

Carter, Steven D. *Traditional Japanese Poetry: An Anthology.* Stanford University Press, 1991.

Carter, Steven D. *Waiting for the Wind: Thirty-Six Poets of Japan's Late Medieval Age.* New York: Columbia University Press, 1989.

Cranston, Edwin A. *A Waka Anthology.* Stanford University Press, 1993.

Kei, M. *Fire Pearls.* Lulu.com, 2006.

Kei, M. *Fire Pearls 2: Short Masterpieces of the Human Heart.* CreateSpace Independent Publishing, 2013.

McClintock, Michael, and Denis M. Garrison. *The Five-Hole Flute: Modern English Tanka in Sequences and Sets.* Baltimore, Maryland: Modern English Tanka Press, 2006.

McClintock, Michael, Pamela Miller Ness, and Jim Kacian. *The Tanka Anthology: Tanka in English from around the World.* Winchester, Virginia: Red Moon Press, 2003.

Miner, Earl Roy, and Robert H. Brower. *An Introduction to Japanese Court Poetry.* Stanford University Press, 1968.

Miner, Earl Roy, and Robert H. Brower. *Japanese Court Poetry*. Stanford University Press, 1961.

Newton, Peter, and Kathe L. Palka. *A Path of Desire: Tan Renga*. Winchester, Virginia: Red Moon Press, 2015.

Reichhold, Jane, and Werner Reichhold. *Wind Five Folded: An Anthology of English-Language Tanka*. Gualala, California: AHA Books, 1994.

St. Maur, Gerald. *Countless Leaves*. Edmonton, Alberta: Inkling Press, 2001.

Tanemura, Kenneth, and A. C. Missias. *New Moon: An Introduction to Issues in Contemporary American Tanka*. Philadelphia, Pennsylvania: Redfox Press, 2001.

Tasker, Brian. *In the Ship's Wake: An Anthology of Tanka*. North Shields: Iron Press, 2001.

Ueda, Makoto. *Modern Japanese Tanka: An Anthology*. New York: Columbia University Press, 1996.

Uzawa, Kozue, and Amelia Fielden. *Ferris Wheel: 101 Modern Contemporary Tanka = Kanransha : Eiyaku gendai tanka 101-shu*. Boston, Massachusetts: Cheng & Tsui Co., 2006.

Ward, Linda Jeannette, Kay Anderson, and Pamela A. Babusci. *Full Moon Tide: The Best of Tanka Splendor, 1990-1999*. Coinjock, North Carolina: Clinging Vine Press, 2000.

Periodicals

Atlas Poetica, A Journal of World Tanka

Blithe Spirit, journal of the British Haiku Society

Eucalypt, Australia's first tanka journal

GUSTS, Canada's first English tanka journal

Kokako, a tanka journal out of New Zealand

Modern English Tanka

Red Lights

Ribbons, journal of the Tanka Society of America

Web Resources

Michael Dylan Welch <www.graceguts.com>

Tanka Canada <tanka.a2hosted.com>

Aha Poetry Forum <forum.ahapoetry.com>

Kyoka Mad Poems Group <groups.google.com/group/kyoka>

American Tanka <www.americantanka.com>

Tanka Society of America <www.tankasocietyofamerica.org>

ABOUT THE AUTHOR

NAOMI BETH WAKAN IS THE INAUGURAL POET
Laureate of Nanaimo (2013-16) and the inaugural Honorary
Ambassador for the Federation of British Columbia Writers.
She has published over fifty books. Her essays are in *Late
Bloomer: On Writing Later in Life*; *Composition, Notes on
the Written Word*; *Book Ends: A Year Between the Covers*;
A Roller-Coaster Ride: Thoughts on Aging (all from Wolsak
and Wynn Publishers); and *On the Arts* (Pacific-Rim
Publishers). Her poetry books include *Sex after 70 and Other
Poems* and *And After 80 . . .* (Bevalia Press) and *Bent Arm
for a Pillow* (Pacific-Rim Publishers). Wakan is a member of
The League of Canadian Poets, Haiku Canada, and Tanka
Canada. She lives on Gabriola Island with her husband, the
sculptor Elias Wakan.

www.naomiwakan.com

Tanka for five rivers

Thames —
did the tall ships leaving
her docks know their future;
whether they would reach
charted ports, let alone
return to safe harbour?

Skeena —
close as sardines in a can
the salmon swim up the Skeena
to make their gravel nests;
then spawning and dying
beginning and ending so close

The Amazon —
the young boy
paddles a load of coconuts
up the mile-wide river
staying close to the bank
he hears small children playing

River Cam —
in a dream
a young man stands punting,
and lying in his boat,
dipping her hand in the water,
a young girl, lethargic with love

Nanaimo River —
at the swimming hole
the boys take turns swinging
out on a rope . . .
it circles wide over the water
as they splash in, it returns